A JOHN CATT PUBLICATION

THE CURRICULUM
Gallimaufry to coherence

Mary Myatt

'An absolutely sizzling synthesis of practical wisdom about curriculum' - David Weston

First Published 2018

by John Catt Educational Ltd,
15 Riduna Park,
Melton, Woodbridge IP12 1QT
Tel: +44 (0) 1394 389850 Fax: +44 (0) 1394 386893
Email: enquiries@johncatt.com
Website: www.johncatt.com

Cover photo by Arif Wahid on Unsplash
With thanks to Sharon Artley for suggesting 'gallimaufry'

Opinions expressed in this publication are those of the contributors
and are not necessarily those of the publishers or the editors.
We cannot accept responsibility for any errors or omissions.

ISBN: 978 1 911382 83 6

Printed and bound in Great Britain

Reviews

'This book weaves together theory, research, policy, and practice to provide educators at every stage of their career a practical guide to coherent curriculum design. Chapters divided by subject and strategy make it easy to keep coming back to, whilst Mary's humorous and intelligent prose make it a pleasure to read.'

Claire Hill, Head of English and Media Studies, Dover Grammar School for Girls

'This book has been invaluable and really balances theory, critical argument and practical applications for how we can achieve this in our curriculum planning and subject CPD.'

Aja Cortizo, Professional Development Team Lead, Glyn School

'This is exactly what I needed to read before the team goes to rewrite the curriculum this term. It is definitely a must-read to completely rethink the curriculum because it covers all aspects to truly ensure 'high challenge and low threat' across all subjects. I'm so excited about redesigning the teaching and learning to ensure children are engaged and inspired.'

Flora Barton, Headteacher, Crowmarsh Gifford CE Primary School

'Globally, new attention is being given to curriculum principles and curriculum practice. Mary Myatt's book is major contribution to this debate. She combines encyclopedic knowledge of schools with crystal-clear description of curriculum principles and few books range so effectively across curriculum theory and day-to-day practice in the classroom. Mary does this with huge authority and extreme clarity. A must-read for all those involved in improving education.'

Tim Oates CBE
Group Director of ARD, Assessment Research and Development,
Cambridge Assessment

'This is an absolutely sizzling synthesis of practical wisdom about curriculum. Rooted in research and punctuated with inspirational examples, Mary has written an accessible and engaging guide to everything that a school needs to know to clarify, deepen and extend its curriculum thinking.'

David Weston, Chief Executive, Teacher Development Trust

This is a book of profound scope. Whether you are a recently qualified teacher or experienced senior leader, there is something in this wonderful book for everyone. The concise structure of the narrative means that, as a reader, it's easy to access and the discourse simple to follow. However, the concepts that the book tackle are by no means 'simple' and all too often it makes you stop and reflect quite critically on everything that you once thought were true of a great curriculum. Mary reminds us that 'we need to pay as much attention to the 'soft' stuff as to the 'hard' metrics'. This is a challenge that we all face in an era of ever-increasing accountability and dwindling resources. For this reason – and for the fact that it is so well-written – Mary's timely new book should be read near and far so that we don't all end up in the proverbial stew.

Andrew Morrish, CEO of Victoria Academies Trust and author of *The Art of Standing Out*

Contents

Foreword 5
Introduction 11

Section 1: Curriculum Fundamentals 12
A brief history of the National Curriculum 13
Curriculum Purpose 17
Curriculum Coherence 20
Subject knowledge 24
Subject knowledge and pupils 29
Cognitive Science 32

Section 2: Curriculum Planning 37
Planning 38
Curriculum Products 41
Beautiful work 44
Curriculum pace 47
Developing expertise 50

Section 3: Assessment and Feedback 53
Assessment 54
Curriculum without levels 57
Feedback and marking 61
On filling the gaps 65
Differentiation 68
Challenge 71

Section 4: Curriculum Instruments 74
Question kleptomaniacs 75
Mastery 78
Intellectual architecture 82
Stimulus 86
Knowledge Organisers 89
Vocabulary 93

Etymology 96
Visits and visitors.. 100

Section 5: Across the Curriculum.. 104
Speaking.. 105
Reading across the curriculum 111
Writing 115
Numeracy across the curriculum.. 120
SMSC across the curriculum.. 124
Planning across the curriculum 128
The hidden curriculum 131

Section 6: Leadership.. 135
Curriculum leadership 136
Accountability 145

Section 7: Subject commentaries 148
Introduction.. 149
Art and Design 152
Computing.. 156
Design and Technology.. 159
English 163
Geography.. 170
History 174
Languages.. 178
Mathematics.. 182
Music 186
Physical Education 190
Religious Education.. 194
Science 197

Foreword

Tom Sherrington

Like all great teachers, Mary Myatt knows how to hook you in and get you thinking. She had me from the title of this marvellous book. Gallimaufry? Ok, I'll admit it. I had to look it up: *a confused jumble or medley of things – such as a stew made of humble ingredients.* Sound familiar? It does to me. The curriculum stew delivered in many of our schools is often the result of rather uncoordinated if noble attempts to squeeze the quart of curriculum demands into the pint-pot of time that makes up a child's school experience. Just think about that vast ocean of knowledge; the ever-growing list of vitally important things that people continually suggest that school should teach – with always just the same amount of time to fit it into.

Getting this right is a massive challenge and, as Mary points out, we need to live with the fact that 'it's never going to be possible to do it all'. However, she's also very clear that gallimaufry isn't good enough. Not if we're serious about providing the 'proper curriculum' that is the entitlement of every child. The goal of 'coherence' is a key theme of the book. If we're going to have to leave things out , the curriculum we do deliver needs to work as a whole with links and threads running through it so that it all makes sense; so that teachers can know how all their various bits of the puzzle fit together across subject domains and over time within each one.

After many years where teachers and leaders have been somewhat side-tracked by discussions of generic pedagogy, overly-nebulous ideas about character and skills whilst also being rather bogged-down in a mire of accountability-driven assessment tracking, we're entering a time where the substance of what is taught is returning to the forefront. In my work its common to find Headteachers who don't know which texts or periods of history are taught in their schools but will know the percentage of students in various subgroups who achieve some nominal standard. That, to me, suggests we've got our priorities wrong.

However, increasingly, across the system, people are talking about knowledge and curriculum, recognising that the solutions to overcoming achievement barriers lie in understanding the curriculum and in what children are meant to know. More schools are reviewing the structure of their curriculum frameworks and are starting to explore ideas about sequencing concepts for maximum success alongside the teaching tools needs to secure knowledge for the long term.

Mary Myatt couches the debates that underpin the review process as a conversation. I love that sense of dialogue and debate that she conveys. In order to reach coherence, it's going to require teachers in schools to engage in the conversation; it's a journey we need to share if we're going to deliver a curriculum we understand and believe in.

Any conversation needs a language everyone can understand and, through a series beautifully lean, crystal-clear chapters, Mary guides us through the key vocabulary we're going to need – the fundamentals and instruments as she calls them. There are a host of concepts that teachers and leaders should be grappling with and using with some fluency if they're going to make good decisions: purpose, coherence, mastery, pace, etymology and the brilliant concept of 'intellectual architecture'. She recognises that many of these ideas have to take from in subject domains. The final section of the book brings the generic elements of the conversation alive with an impressive array of examples from across the curriculum with lots of helpful, practical links for further reading.

Crucially, this book is much more than a being a neutral, factual guide; it's laced throughout with her campaigning zeal – a call to arms from someone with a genuine conviction that curriculum matters a great deal. If we're going to ensure that 'the marvels and the jewels' in our curriculum form an entitlement 'for the many' this is a conversation that is necessary; important; urgent. In her timely book, Mary makes it clear that the curriculum conversations we need to have should be driven by that vision. Inspiring and helpful in equal measure, this book is going to make a significant contribution to the work schools need to do to make the vision a reality.

Tom Sherrington

Former teacher and headteacher;
consultant and author of *The Learning Rainforest*

For Brian. And Tess

Introduction

This book is meant as a starter for discussion about the curriculum, not to be the last word. 'Gallimaufry' has been chosen to capture the mixed picture as it currently stands in relation to the curriculum in much of the sector. It is fair to say that the 'stuff' of curriculum content for subjects has been lost over the years, and now is the time for leaders to have real purchase on the quality and coherence of what their pupils are studying.

In the brief history of the National Curriculum, I trace the story of how we have come to the current version for schools. In the rest of the book, the main thrust of my argument is that a proper curriculum, grounded in the knowledge, concepts and overarching ideas of individual subjects is an entitlement for every child. A second strand of the book is that the curriculum we offer our children, through the lessons we teach, should be appropriately demanding: that we shouldn't be tempted to dumb material down in a mistaken belief that our pupils can't cope. It is our job to help them to reach into the marvels and the jewels which are contained within our curriculum. This is not an entitlement for the few, but for the many.

The book has seven sections: the first covers the history and some of the fundamental principles of a curriculum; the second is on planning; the third, assessment and feedback; the fourth covers some of the elements we need to include to make the curriculum really robust; the fifth considers elements which go across the curriculum; the sixth, some guidance for leaders and the final section on subjects is written as prompts and starters for conversations and includes links for resources and further ideas. Here's to an honest, and careful conversation about what a really robust curriculum looks like for all our pupils.

Mary Myatt, May 2018

Section 1: Curriculum Fundamentals

A brief history of the National Curriculum

'The job of a good curriculum is to inspire teachers, not instruct them.'
Russell Hobby

The National Curriculum was introduced in England, Wales and Northern Ireland as a nationwide curriculum for primary and secondary state schools following the Education Reform Act (1988).[1] Before the introduction of a national curriculum, local authorities or schools decided school curricula. While some educational content was high-quality, findings primarily from the inspectorate found that, for many pupils, this was not the case.[2] The National Curriculum of 1988 set out 'attainment targets' – the knowledge, skills and understanding which children would be expected to have by the end of each key stage, the 'programmes of study' to be taught at each key stage and the arrangements for assessing pupils at the end of each key stage.[3]

---

1   The National Curriculum does not apply to Northern Ireland and Wales since devolution. It also does not apply to academies and free schools.
2   www.educationengland.org.uk/documents/des/framework-1980.html
3   www.legislation.gov.uk/ukpga/1988/40/contents

The need for a national curriculum was anticipated by Sir Jim Callaghan's 'Great Debate'[4] speech at Ruskin College in 1976. In arguing for an entitlement for all pupils, Callaghan made the case for a 'core curriculum of basic knowledge.' He argued that education should 'equip children for a lively, constructive place in society, and also to fit them to do a job of work.' While the Ruskin speech put the National Curriculum on the political agenda for the first time, it was the Education Reform Act of 1988 which turned it into reality.

There have been a number of revisions to the National Curriculum since 1988, mostly intended to simplify and slim down the content. The prelude to the current curriculum started with the coalition government in 2010. The 2007 changes were shelved and an expert review panel was commissioned to report on a framework for a new National Curriculum. This was led by Tim Oates and reported in December 2011. The government produced a final version in September 2013, for first teaching in maintained schools from September 2014, with the expectation that it would be taught to all year groups from September 2015. Free schools and academies do not have to follow the National Curriculum, but as a requirement of their funding agreements, the curriculum needs to be broad and balanced and they have an obligation to provide English, maths and science as well as religious education.

In 2010, Tim Oates' paper 'Could do better – using international comparisons to refine the National Curriculum in England'[5] established the principles for the review. The background research for this paper found that those countries and jurisdictions which have the highest levels of pupil and student outcomes are characterised by a clear rationale for what is to be taught and explicit subject content to be covered. Again, there was an ambition to slim down curriculum content: 'The reduction in bulk is important; there is strong evidence of teachers moving with undue, enforced pace through an overladen curriculum ... deep learning must be a principal goal of the national curriculum, with learners able to retain and transfer learning.[6] For this to occur, adequate time on topics must be possible. This is not an argument against adequate pace and progression.

---

4   www.educationengland.org.uk/documents/speeches/1976ruskin.html
5   Oates, T. (2011) Could do better: using international comparisons to refine the National Curriculum in England, *The Curriculum Journal*, 22 (2), 121-150, DOI: 10.1080/09585176.2011.578908
6   Black, P., & Wiliam, D. (1998) *Children, Schools and Families Committee 2009*

It is a recognition that an overblown curriculum specification can give rise to undue pace, and that undue pace erodes deep learning, promotes a 'tick box' approach to learning amongst both teachers and learners, and compromises genuine accumulation of learning (characterised by retention and redeployment of knowledge and skills.')

On the basis of international comparisons, the paper argued that 'a well-defined and enhanced national curriculum, based on concepts, principles, fundamental operations and key knowledge can lead to learning processes which are more focused on deep learning with fewer topics pursued to greater depth, and to assessment processes of greater validity and which have beneficial wash back into learning.'[7]

The new curriculum also removed levels. Oates' work had identified a number of problems with the use of levels. Their original purpose had been to indicate what a child of seven, eleven or fourteen might reasonably be expected to achieve by the end of a key stage. What happened in practice was that the levels became overcomplicated and drifted far from their original purpose. For example, the use of levels for accountability – schools, local authorities and Ofsted all paying close attention to the percentage of children who had reached the end of key stage levels. This put further pressure on teachers to hurry their children through the content.

The end result of the latest iteration of the curriculum was intended to be a slimmed down curriculum, focusing on key ideas and concepts, which are essential for learning in any particular subject. At the start of each of the subjects in the National Curriculum is the introductory purpose of study and aims. These set out the rationale for teaching this subject to pupils and have been written to ensure that the key messages are clear. What follows the objectives are the fundamental ideas and material to be taught for each key stage. Apart from English and mathematics, the material can be taught in any order. The attainment targets show what pupils are expected to know, apply and understand from the relevant programme of study.

'The National Curriculum' and 'the curriculum' should not be confused – it is vital to distinguish between them. The curriculum – taught and untaught -represents the totality of the experience of the child within schooling (aims, content, pedagogy, assessment). It includes wider

---

7   Oates *op. cit.*

elements, including opportunities to acquire vital 'personal' and 'social' capitals. A national curriculum cannot specify and control all elements of the 'real' curriculum and is likely to run into difficulty if it attempts so to do. A national curriculum operates as a means of giving all pupils access to a common body of essential content.

And so, how has the latest National Curriculum been enacted? Well, some parts well and others not so. For many schools, the pressure of ensuring that pupils meet the expected standards at the end of Key Stage 2 has often squeezed out the wider, rich range of subjects to which they are entitled in order to focus on English and maths. Similarly, in many secondary schools, the focus on pupils' achievement at the end of Key Stage 4 has meant a diminished diet for many at Key Stage 3. While the reasons for a restricted curriculum are understandable, it is nevertheless important that schools revisit their rationale for what they provide for their pupils.

A further problem is that the aims and objectives within the National Curriculum subjects are often only skimmed, if at all, and the focus goes straight to the detail of what needs to be taught. This misses the point. What needs to be taught needs to be set in the context of a bigger picture, informed by the purpose and aims. The National Curriculum is not a scheme of work; it is a framework, which allows for considerable contextualising.

To summarise: there are three important things to keep in mind about the curriculum. The first is that it is both more complex and simpler than we have come to think. The second is that its status and content now have a higher profile than in recent years. And the third is that it is never going to be possible to do it all. And we need to live with that.

Curriculum purpose

'The foundation of every state is the education of its youth.'
Diogenes

Why a section on purpose? Well, it is important to think about it from two aspects: first, what is the purpose of a national curriculum and second, how do we ensure that what we teach has a wider meaning?

To answer the first: the purpose of a national curriculum is to set out the principles, aims and the content of the subjects to be studied by pupils across their time in primary and secondary schooling. It is a way of ensuring that all pupils encounter, engage with and study to varying degrees of depth, the content and material which are considered important for a rounded education. It sets out the stall for the range of goodies to which all young people in maintained schools in England are entitled. There is a lot of talk about entitlement and it means this – that we are depriving our young people of intellectual, artistic and physical nourishment if they are not given proper access to these. And that means that they have a right to education which is well-taught, well-resourced and properly funded.

While the first purpose is political and economical, the second purpose is more philosophical. It links in part to curriculum cohesion in terms of supporting a framework for thinking about how it is planned and delivered – however, it is also more than this. It asks the questions, why am I teaching this lesson? What are my pupils meant to make of it? What is it for? Now when we start asking these questions, our answers tell us something very important about the nature of our planning and thinking about the curriculum. There are a number of superficial answers to the question, why am I teaching this lesson:

- Because I have been timetabled to teach it.
- No idea, they are someone else's plans.
- They are needed for the SATS or GCSEs.

But the question deserves a bigger, more robust answer. There are several levels of 'why' beyond the superficial. It should take us a moment or two to ask ourselves, actually why am I teaching this? Where does it fit into the bigger picture of the curriculum plans? Why is it important to know this or master it? What difference would it make to the learning if we didn't do this lesson? If we take the trouble to do this every lesson, it will do several things – it will locate our own thinking and planning into the bigger whole, it will often remind us of why we are teaching this subject, it will help us to make links with what has gone before, or will anticipate what is still to come. It will also act as a checklist: do I really need to do this? What will it add?

One of the main reasons for asking why we are teaching something is so that we can make those links very clear to children. We are learning this today, so that we:

- can work out...
- see how this connects with...
- are familiar with this, because we will come across it often

Providing the reasons stops us from breaking the content into atomised sections which are taught in isolation. If we aren't careful, we teach a series of lessons about things which not only bear no relation to one another, but which have not been explained to children. So, a lesson on partition, for instance, is unlikely to make sense to children if they have not been given the purpose of learning about partition. What happens is that they learn ad hoc strategies to do partition, but without any of the underlying understanding of primarily what partition is supposed to do and why it might be important to know how to do it. There are too many children who, when asked what they are doing and why, turn back to the board to read from the learning objective. When asked what this is in their own words, they aren't able to say. This is a crying shame and means that the lesson has pretty much been a waste of time. They might have completed a few exercises in their books, but are unable to do so either autonomously or with confidence. All because they have not been told the purpose of what they are doing.

When done well, however, and on a regular basis, it transforms lessons from routine completion of tasks to deep understanding. When this happens, the teacher has most likely gone through something like the following: 'We are learning about this today. It is important to know about this because... and it will help us to...' This is a form of Zoe Elder's structure which states that 'we are learning this... so that...'[1] Essentially, this stops things from going adrift and losing structure and purpose. All our children ought to be able to tell us what they are learning about and why it is important. If they can't, we haven't taught them properly.

Perhaps, best of all, it injects a spirit of enjoyment into the lesson. If we can see where this links to the wider picture, we can often make other connections which make sense and are often enjoyable. So, to go back to the lesson on partition, the children who had pretty much no idea what they were doing would have had a completely different relationship with the material if they had had a few minutes to talk through what partition meant, where the word came from and why it is a useful/essential thing to be able to do in maths. They might have made the connection with separating things into parts, dividing up and perhaps have brought some of their own examples of when things had been divided or split up when they were sharing sweets or biscuits with their friends. A simple connection, but one which would have made the purpose and connection clear from the start.

---

1   fullonlearning.com/2012/10/01/constructing-learning-so-that-it-is-meaningful-and-purposeful

Curriculum coherence

'When the curriculum lacks coherence, it is both harder to teach and harder for children to locate and place their new knowledge.'
Viviane Robinson

There are three aspects to curriculum coherence. The first is national, the second is at school level and the third, where the real work is, is at classroom level. This is where it will have greatest impact for pupils.

Let's take the first, at national level. Curriculum coherence was identified by Tim Oates in 'Could do better'[1] as one of the characteristics of high performing jurisdictions: 'The weight of evidence from transnational comparison is that a certain degree of curriculum control is necessary (that this need not be associated with "top down" control or control exercised exclusively by the State) and that this control should be directed towards attaining "curriculum coherence."' He goes on to say 'The term "coherence" does not carry the meaning typically associated

---

1   Could do better: using international comparisons to refine the National
    Curriculum in England: www.youtube.com/watch?v=-q5vrBXFpm0

with a "broad and balanced curriculum" but is a precise technical term: a national curriculum should have content arranged in an order which is securely based in evidence associated with age-related progression, and all elements of the system (content, assessment, pedagogy, teacher training, teaching materials, incentives and drivers etc) should all line up and act in a concerted way to deliver public goods' (Schmidt & Prawat[2]). This is not just a trivial, common-language use of the term 'coherence'. A system is regarded as 'coherent' when the national curriculum content, textbooks, teaching content, pedagogy, assessment and drivers and incentives all are aligned and reinforce one another. '...Curricular materials in high-performing nations focus on fewer topics, but also communicate the expectation that those topics will be taught in a deeper, more profound way.'[3]

A similar case is made by Michael Young in 'Towards a subject based curriculum'[4] where the argument is that, at both national and school level, the curriculum should be based on a number of principles. First, its purpose must be the intellectual development of pupils in the range of core subjects. Second, the National Curriculum should be subject-based, because for schools, progression in subjects is the most reliable way of defining the individual development of students. Third, it must stipulate each subject's core concepts and only the content related to these concepts. Fourth, it must clearly distinguish the curriculum – at both national and school levels – from pedagogy.'

The second location for coherence is at school leadership level. Curriculum planning consists of more than organizing a timetable. It is about leaders having thoughtful conversations with colleagues about the curriculum map for the pupils in their school. It means paying careful attention to how the material to be studied is organised. Curriculum planning means rethinking topic work and the muddle that was possible, although not inevitable, from 'topics' with titles such as water or colour. Unless such vague topics are underpinned by a clear rationale and conceptual rigour, they devolve into ridiculous, tenuous links. One example, described by Christine Counsell in Clare Sealy's blog, is a history

2   Schmidt, W. & Prawat, R. (2006) 'Curriculum coherence and national control of education: issue or non-issue?' *Journal of Curriculum Studies*, 38 (6) pp. 641-658
3   *op. cit.* p.1
4   academyofideas.org.uk/documents/educationforum/Towards_a_subject_based_education_IOI_Ed_Forum_April_2012.pdf

teacher, desperate to link the theme of colour, including a topic on the Black Death.[5] Or a theme on water, where in religious education, this gets translated into Jesus walking on water. And yes, he probably would have wept. While these examples are amusing, they are doing a real disservice to pupils' cognitive development. And so, for example, children asked about what they had learnt in history returned blank looks. Prompted about work they had done on the Ancient Greeks, one child piped up, 'Oh no that wasn't history, that was "Topic."' Well, quite.

These are prime examples of the integrity of subjects being degraded. This is not to say that links across a curriculum are not possible and cannot provide additional richness and complexity to a subject, rather that we need to think: what is the main idea we want pupils to think about?

Thinking hard about coherence matters, because if we don't, then what is offered to children is bitty. Bitty means that there are lots of fragments of knowledge floating around without being placed in a bigger basket. And so a rationale is needed. This is clearly articulated in the National Curriculum – at the start of each subject area to be taught is a clear statement for the big picture. This needs to be held in mind when constructing long and medium-term plans and also in the daily delivering of lessons. It takes just a few moments to remind our pupils and ourselves of the connection between what is being taught and learnt today and the bigger picture. This is both more satisfying and effective. It is more satisfying because everyone can see how the learning today relates to a bigger story and it is more effective because the detail of today is more likely to stick when put into the context of the overall scheme.

There is a second strand to curriculum coherence at school level and it is this: careful attention needs to be paid to the underlying knowledge which pupils need in order to access the subject in later years. A good example of this is an English department at Dover Grammar School for Girls where Claire Hill is Head of English and Media Studies. She and her colleagues have identified the biblical and classical allusions needed in order to study 'Macbeth', for example, and have included these in a unit for Key Stage 3. Working in this careful, structured way is light years away from scrappy, ad hoc lessons, which do not create the opportunities and expectations for pupils to be *au fait* with essential background knowledge.

---

5   primarytimery.com/2017/10/28/the-3d-curriculum-that-promotes-remembering

We are a pattern-seeking species. We look to make sense and order from the world around us. The plethora of information and stimuli become overwhelming if each is encountered without a context into which to place it. From our earliest days, man has sorted information in order to categorise the world. This is an efficient way of staying alive. Noticing that some things support life and others are likely to endanger it is an essential aspect of human survival. Recognising plants and berries and identifying those which gave nourishment and those which were likely to kill us, were essentials in keeping the species alive.

Our fascination with the world and the skies is linked to our seeking pattern and order. So, it is hard-wired into us to want to see how things connect. And this idea should be fundamental to thinking about a curriculum and its coherence. Coherence comes from the Latin 'to stick together', and when we think about the curriculum coherently, it becomes much simpler to teach and for pupils to understand. And the coherence comes from paying attention to the big ideas which underpin each curriculum area. These have not been written as a pretty piece of prose by way of introduction, but are the essential 'meme' through which the detail is expressed. The temptation is to go straight to the detail of what needs to be taught. And this is understandable when we are under time pressure. But in the long term, we waste time because we have not invested in two things: identifying the key ideas and concepts, and not sharing these with our pupils. This means we are denying them the chance to get the material to stick together.

When the curriculum lacks coherence, it is both harder to teach and harder for children to locate and place their new knowledge. Each of the subject areas of the National Curriculum has two sections at the start before going into the detail: first the purpose. This sets out the reason why this subject needs to be taught and the impact of teaching it on pupils. The purpose is followed by the aims and sets out the entitlement for all pupils. Combined, these provide a platform both for thinking about and making sense of the curriculum detail and for ensuring that every child has access to it.

Subject knowledge

'Knowledge is power.
Information is liberating.'
Kofi Anan

Let's start with a thought experiment. As the owner of a restaurant, you spend a great deal of time making sure that your customers have a good experience. So, you make sure that you pay attention to the different aspects of your business: you make sure that the front of house is welcoming, that the tables are well-presented, staff well-trained, health and safety standards met, the kitchen is clean and so on. But for some reason, you don't think it is important to check the quality of the ingredients. You just assume that the chef will know what to do, that she doesn't need support and that it is irrelevant whether she is in touch with the latest thinking.

I think it would become clear fairly quickly that there was something wrong. While the quality of the food reaching the table is ok, the ingredients are not as fresh or clear-cut as they might be. In fact, it's all a bit stale. Let's be clear: this is not the chef's fault. You, as restaurant owner, have not checked that the quality of what is going into the dishes is as fresh and as high-quality as it could be. Why? Because in this thought experiment, you were caught up and busy with the ephemera, without going back to basics and making sure that the core ingredients, namely the raw materials, were of sufficient quality.

This thought experiment is a way of thinking about how subject knowledge and subject expertise have been treated across the sector. There are some settings where subject knowledge development has been a high priority, but they have been the exception rather than the rule. This is not to blame leaders for the current lack of focus on subject knowledge, but rather to shine a light on how we got here.

It is fair to say that a number of factors have clouded the focus on developing teachers' subject knowledge. An over-emphasis on generic aspects of school life, such as marking and feedback, for example, assumed that secure subject knowledge on the part of the teacher was a given. Similarly, there have been unholy contortions trying to fit generic skills into the highly diverse subject structures; again, a mistake to think that progress looks the same across all subjects. It is fair to say that parts of the sector have been seduced by ephemera or showy lessons which may or may not have had substance, a misplaced focus on whether pupils were engaged and what it would take for them to be engaged. What followed from this was that many lessons were distorted in order to produce pseudo 'wow' factors, superficial activities which valued whizziness over substance, prettiness over content and 'box office' over scholarly work.

And then again, much subject CPD has been limited to exam changes at GCSE and A level. This has meant that a lack of imagination and an instrumentalist view of education have seen such training as important to get pupils through exams. The default model has been for one teacher to attend a course and return to 'cascade' to colleagues. This is hardly continuing professional development. Much provision for subject knowledge development at primary and Key Stage 3 has been run down. This is due in part to the slimming down of local authorities, many of which used to provide regular networks, conferences and courses to support professional knowledge, and as a result, many of these are no longer running.

It is important to emphasise that there are some schools and groups of schools where the sidelining of the curriculum beyond English and maths in primary and a distortion at Key Stage 3 in secondary has not been the case.

In some areas, schools are working together, subject specialists within an MAT are providing resources and training and subject associations are building capacity, but this is *ad hoc* to say the least.

It is important that the development of subject knowledge moves up the pecking order of competing school priorities. And the reason for this, at its heart, is that it is an entitlement for pupils to have an honest curriculum, not one which is distorted by a misplaced focus on accountability measures.

There are two aspects to subject knowledge and the first is teacher knowledge. We cannot possibly know everything we are expected to teach and so we have an obligation to keep in touch with the latest thinking on curriculum developments. Subject associations such as the Historical Association[1] bring together the latest scholarship in, for instance, medieval history and show how this can be used in lessons. As Philippa Cordingley's work has found, teachers say that they find subject-specific continuing professional development more beneficial to their teaching than generic pedagogic CPD – and the evidence suggests that they are right in this judgement. It seems strange then, that teachers in the UK generally do less subject-specific CPD than generic CPD and less, also, than their colleagues in high-performing countries.[2] One way to audit this is to use the CPD Quality Audit from the Teacher Development Trust.[3]

The second aspect of subject knowledge is what pupils are expected to know. They will not know and understand material unless it is made explicit, they are expected to learn it, are tested on it (via low stakes tests) and have the chance to produce something which gives an indication of the extent to which they have mastered the knowledge. This cannot be done through random worksheets, which have a tendency to fill a space rather than being part of a coherent whole. We need to stop being squeamish about talking about scholarship, deep learning and our pupils having access to and mastering robust knowledge.

Michael Young, Professor of Education at UCL Unstitute of Education, has argued for the right of all children and young people to be taught what he terms 'powerful knowledge'. He makes the distinction that this 'is not knowledge of the powerful; rather powerful knowledge comes from specialist communities and centuries of learning, and it does change, but much more slowly than people believe. It is context-independent. It can lift children and young people out of their lived experience. And this is

---

1   www.history.org.uk
2   www.curee.co.uk/file/5349
3   tdtrust.org/cpd-quality-audit

not to decry that experience. It is the job of the teacher to engage with the prior experience of pupils and to give them access to the powerful knowledge.'[4]

As Carolyn Roberts, headteacher at Thomas Tallis School, says, 'schools share powerful knowledge on behalf of society so we teach them what they need to know to make sense of and to improve the world. They need that knowledge in order to interpret and improve the world. It enables them to grow into useful citizens. It enables them to grow into citizens who understand one another. It's fair and just that all children should have access to this kind of learning and this kind of knowledge.'[5]

She summarises her school's philosophy in this powerful *aide-memoire*:

1. Knowledge is worthwhile in itself. Tell children this: never apologise that you need to learn things.
2. Schools transmit shared and powerful knowledge on behalf of society. We teach what they need to make sense of and improve the world.
3. Shared and powerful knowledge is verified through learned communities. We need to keep in touch with universities, research and subject associations.
4. Children need powerful knowledge to understand and interpret the world. Without it they remain dependent upon those who have it.
5. Powerful knowledge is cognitively superior to that needed for daily life. It transcends and liberates children from their daily experience.
6. Shared and powerful knowledge enables children to grow into useful citizens. As adults they can understand, cooperate and shape the world together.
7. Shared knowledge is a foundation for a just and sustainable democracy. Citizens educated together share an understanding of the common good.
8. It is fair and just that all children should have access to this knowledge. Powerful knowledge opens doors: it must be available to all children.

---

4   www.cambridgeassessment.org.uk/insights/the-attack-on-knowledge
5   policyexchange.org.uk/event/creating-a-powerful-knowledge-curriculum-in-schools

9. Accepted adult authority is required for shared knowledge transmission. The teacher's authority to transmit knowledge is given and valued by society.
10. Pedagogy links adult authority, powerful knowledge and its transmission. We need quality professionals to achieve all of this for all our children.

Subject knowledge and pupils

'Knowledge begets knowledge.'
E. D. Hirsch

Our pupils need to know stuff and the minimum standards for that stuff are expressed in the National Curriculum documents for each subject. There is no getting away from this for maintained schools. Academies and free schools are able to determine their own curriculum, but the obligation is still to ensure that it is broad and balanced.

However, the main question is, do our pupils know, really know, on their own terms, the key aspects of a topic in history, geography or whatever subject? Are they capable of producing something worthwhile as a result of acquiring that knowledge? In other words, are they creating something with what they have been taught or are they consumers of worksheets?

There are two strands which need strengthening in relation to pupils' subject knowledge. The first is that in the past, there has been too much emphasis on skills development. Skills are important, but they do not stand alone as aspects of learning, separate from knowledge. So, for example, pupils have been given a piece of prose to read and then asked what they 'infer' from the text without discussion or support to understand that there is often much implied behind a text which is not explicitly written or spoken. This is sophisticated work. It is like peering through the shadows to glimpse at more information. It is there, but it is subtle. And just telling pupils that it is there is not the same as supporting them to find what is there. Sometimes, mistakenly, the text is regarded as less important than the 'skill' of inference. But it is the text which is the locus of inference: it is the text itself which provides the clues, it is knowing what the text is communicating beyond the actual statements, what it might be hinting at, what might be implied, or what might be inferred. It is the text which is of primary importance and the capacity to infer can only come from deep engagement with that text. The same mistake happens with comprehension. The capacity to understand the material in a text does not stand separately from the text. We cannot assume that focusing just on the skill of comprehension is going to get our pupils to understand or comprehend any other text. The two examples here of inference and comprehension can only emerge through the engagement with lots of material. We cannot say that, because a child can make inferences from one piece of prose, they are equally able to do it from another. Similarly with comprehension. And this is because the skills are closely bound to the subject matter of the text. So, if we are concerned that our pupils' skills in inference and comprehension need to be developed, we should not be focusing on these skills without exposing them to lots of different texts.

Daniel Willingham and Gail Lovette researched the impact of comprehension instruction.[1] What they found was that explicit instruction to pupils – to get them to focus on finding the meaning and to ask questions about a text – improved their comprehension and inference capacity, but that continuing to teach comprehension did not have an impact. They argue that teaching comprehension and inference is useful, but only up to a point. And this is because they are not transferable skills. It doesn't follow that if I understand and can infer from a novel, that I am able to do the same from a news report. So, we need to conclude from this that while instruction and support to comprehend and infer are important, they are always bound to the material in hand. This is why pupils need to read and be read to a lot, so that they have practice in these important skills across a wide range of material. If, as Willingham argues, 'comprehension is highly text-specific and

---

1   www.danielwillingham.com/daniel-willingham-science-and-education-blog/
     infer-this

dependent on background knowledge'[2] then we need to make sure that our pupils have plenty of knowledge. This is echoed in Hirsch's book 'Cultural Literacy' written in 1987. The idea that what separates good readers from poor readers, once we get beyond the mechanics of instruction and phonics, is their background knowledge.

And where are the skills in all this? Well, the skills do not stand alone; they are context-dependent and draw on the content. It is not possible to evaluate or analyse material without knowing the facts. The facts are the building blocks not just of cumulative knowledge over time, but supplying the means with which to interrogate and discuss. Separating the skills from the content has meant a focus on, for example, inference, without providing plenty of examples from which the capacity to infer emerges.

Knowing things helps us to know more things. Knowing things helps us to connect with previous knowledge and to make connections. Knowing things makes us feel clever. When we take short-cuts with knowledge in order to move on to the acquisition of skills, it is like expecting a cook to make a meal with only one ingredient. It takes a range of materials or ingredients to produce something worthwhile.

Linked to this is the knowledge and use of subject-specific terminology which supports pupils to enter the domain of the academic discipline. Each subject has its own vocabulary, which is used specifically within that subject. In geography, for example, erosion has a particular meaning and this meaning needs to be taught explicitly, practised and used on a regular basis. In history, we might identify civilisation, in religious education, worship, and so on. It is an entitlement for pupils to know what these words mean, how they fit into what they are studying and for them to use them with confidence. All pupils like feeling accomplished and it's paying them a compliment to induct them into the knowledge of a particular subject.

And finally, we know that there is a significant word gap between those pupils from advantaged backgrounds and some, not all, from disadvantaged backgrounds by the time they start school.[3] There is nothing we can do about this, but we can do something about it the minute they come into our classrooms. Knowing stuff makes a difference.

---

2   *op. cit.*
3   Hart, B. & Risley, T. (2003): www.aft.org/sites/default/files/periodicals/ TheEarlyCatastrophe.pdf

Cognitive science

'Cognitive psychology has shown that the mind best understands facts when they are woven into a conceptual fabric, such as a narrative, mental map, or intuitive theory. Disconnected facts in the mind are like unlinked pages on the web: they might as well not exist.'

Stephen Pinker

What can cognitive science contribute to our thinking about the curriculum? Plenty. This section takes some of the key messages from cognitive science to help frame our thinking about the curriculum. First, Willingham,[1] next Sweller et al[2] and finally Brown et al.[3] There are plenty more, but these will serve our purpose in helping to get purchase on creating a curriculum which is appropriately demanding and engaging.

---

1   Willingham, D. (2010) *Why Don't Students Like School?* Jossey-Bass.
2   Sweller, J., Ayres, P. & Kalyuga, S. (2011) *Cognitive Load Theory*, Springer.
3   Brown, P., Roediger, H. & McDaniel, M. (2014) *Make It Stick*, Harvard University Press.

First, Willingham argues that humans are hard-wired for stories. 'The human mind seems exquisitely tuned to understand and remember stories – so much so that psychologies sometimes refer to stories as 'psychologically privileged', in that stories are treated differently in the memory compared with other types of material.' Stories provide ways of framing the detail into part of a whole. Stories draw us in. They have many features which have applications for thinking about the curriculum. They create an overarching narrative, are open to a number of interpretations, provide material about which we can ask questions and are often open-ended. Given that we can't learn everything, nor can our pupils, Willingham argues that we should create the conditions for pupils to learn the concepts that come up again and again; what he calls 'the unifying ideas of each discipline... knowledge pays off when facts are related to one another, and that is not true of list learning.' Good teachers are able to 'organise the material in a way that makes it interesting and easy to understand.'

Similarly, Christine Counsell argues that we should think of 'the curriculum as continuous. Not just a sequence or a chronology, it's much more like a narrative. Curriculum is content structured *as narrative* over time... This is because narrative (I mean a good one) has the effect of keeping multiple strands all spinning at once. Thus earlier stages stay warm in memory so that they form part of the backcloth through which we interpret every new element. A narrative is constantly unifying, pulling things together so that they function.'[4]

So how do these headlines translate into curriculum planning? I think there are two strands: the first is that we need to have a clear picture of the overall provision map for each subject across each year. And to ask ourselves, does this provide coherence and is it possible to tell it as a story or narrative? The second element, which follows from this, is that, as pupils begin each unit, they need to know how it fits into the wider whole, so that they can see, appreciate and learn the particular by locating it in the general.

The second takeaway from Willingham's work is that 'solving problems brings pleasure.'[5] Problem-solving here means any cognitive work that succeeds – it might be understanding a difficult passage of prose, or completing a demanding maths problem. 'There is a sense of satisfaction,

4   thedignityofthethingblog.wordpress.com
5   Willingham *op. cit.*

of fulfilment, in successful thinking'.[6] Neuroscientists have made the link between the brain areas and chemicals that are important to learning and those that are important in the brain's natural reward system.[7] When you solve a problem, it appears that the brain rewards itself with a small dose of dopamine and releases a feeling of pleasure. In other words, people take pleasure in solving problems. And it appears that the pleasure is closely related to the solving of the problem. Working on something that appears to have no solution and where we do not seem to make progress is frustrating. And at the opposite end of the spectrum, knowing the answer doesn't result in pleasure. Willingham also points out that if we are given too many hints about a possible solution, we lose the sense that we have solved the problem and 'getting the answer doesn't bring the same mental snap of satisfaction.'

It emerges from this that we like and indeed seek out problems that pose some challenge but have the hope of being solvable, because this brings us feelings of pleasure and satisfaction. 'For problems to be solved, the thinker needs adequate information from the environment, room in working memory and the required facts and procedures in long-term memory.' It seems reasonable that we should think about curriculum design as providing opportunities for these to take place. 'Our curiosity is provoked when we perceive a problem that we believe we can solve. What is the question that will engage students and make them want to know the answer?' When considering 'problems' these are more than simple quizzes, rather they involve 'cognitive work which involves moderate challenge.'

Next, Willingham argues that pupils can't learn everything, so what should they know? Cognitive science suggests that pupils ought to learn the concepts that come up again and again – the unifying ideas of each discipline. Knowledge pays off when it is conceptual and when the facts are related to one another.

Linked to this is the fact that we remember material more easily if we know something about it. If we know some things about a topic, we are able to understand new information about that topic more quickly. Willingham gives the example of how people who know about baseball understand a

6   op. cit.
7   www.theguardian.com/science/2014/oct/02/curiosity-memory-brain-reward-system-dopamine

baseball story better than people who don't. The amount of knowledge of baseball determined how much they understood of the story – whether they were strong or weak readers did not matter as much as what they already knew about baseball. We remember much better if the material we are studying has meaning. So background knowledge needs to be acquired before we can deploy critical thinking skills. A number of studies have shown that people understand what they read much better if they already have some background knowledge about the subject. Researchers Donna Recht and Lauren Leslie carried out a study on reading comprehension.[8] Half the group were poor readers and half were good readers. Researchers asked them to read a story that described a baseball game. The amount of knowledge of baseball determined how much they understood of the story – whether they were strong or weak readers did not matter as much as what they already knew about baseball.

The implication of this for curriculum design is that our pupils need to know a lot of background 'stuff' in order for them to understand the topic in question. This stuff needs to be planned for and thought about carefully. This is because background knowledge helps to create chunking, or an internal picture of what is going on, and, importantly, this is located in the long-term memory, creating more space in the working memory, which is less likely to become overloaded. And so, it is important for curriculum planning to know that it is easier to remember material if we already know something about the topic. We are better able to understand new information and also to remember it, if it has meaning.

The second strand of cognitive science is cognitive load theory via Sweller *et al.*[9] Their extensive research concludes that working memory only has so much capacity for holding and dealing with information. When this is overloaded, pupils find it hard to make sense of both existing and new information. Long-term memory, on the other hand is the foundation for incorporating and making sense of new knowledge. Material sits in the long-term memory when it has been 'chunked', or sorted, into meaningful schemata or concepts. It helps us make sense of new material when the links are either spotted or made explicit. What happens currently, is that the curriculum is often gobbetised into small sections. Pupils are often taught disparate, unconnected material, without any effort being made

8   eric.ed.gov/?id=EJ384774
9   www.springer.com/gb/book/9781441981257

to ensure that it goes into the long-term memory. As a result, something which they might have been taught in the past is forgotten, because pupils have not had the chance to make the links with the overarching material. Planning a curriculum which draws the threads between the overarching ideas and the detail is the key to unlocking the present distance between what is taught and how well it is remembered.

David Brown and colleagues argue in 'Making it Stick' that learning is a three-step process – 'initial encoding of information is held in short-term working memory before being consolidated not a cohesive representation of knowledge in long-term memory. Consolidation reorganises and stabilises memory traces, gives them meaning and makes connections to past experiences and to other knowledge already stored in long-term memory. Retrieval updates learning and enables pupils to apply it when they need it.'[10]

To summarise these insights into school practice, we must do the following: we need to find the stories in the curriculum, we need to think about how we ensure that information moves from the short-term into the long-term memory and we need to provide opportunities for pupils to revisit the key concepts. Clare Sealy has written about how her school revisits the concept of tyranny across different year groups. It's worth quoting in full: 'We first meet a "tyrant" in year 1, when our students encounter King John (of Magna Carta fame) and learn that he was (until the barons got him) a tyrant. We don't meet any tyrants in history again until in year 5 when we encounter Dionysius of Syracuse (the definitive tyrant) where his tyranny is counterpoised with the democracy of Ancient Greek city states. While it's quite a stretch to expect that children will remember the word "tyrant" from 4 years previously, it provides an opportunity to remind students about the Magna Carta and how power is limited in Britain. Then in year 6, we can compare Hitler with Churchill. By now, we also know the adjective "tyrannical."'[11]

---

10   www.hup.harvard.edu/catalog.php?isbn=9780674729018
11   primarytimery.com/2017/10/28/the-3d-curriculum-that-promotes-remembering

Section 2: Curriculum Planning

Curriculum planning

'A good plan is like a road map: it shows the final destination and usually the best way to get there.'
H. Stanley Judd

Planning is critical and it is fundamental in providing the structure and architecture for pupils' learning. Results are better when teachers are given time to plan together on a scheme. This should identify the 'what' and the 'why' of the content to be taught. Best practice in planning starts with an overarching question, ideas for opening up the content and the things to be taught over the medium term. These constitute the big picture and framework for what is to be taught. They are the roadmap. This is a useful metaphor for thinking about the curriculum to be taught. A roadmap shows the destination, but provides a number of routes to get there. This allows for teachers' autonomy in the delivery of the scheme as it unfolds, lesson by lesson. When good-quality schemes of work are in place, they should reduce teacher workload.

The Department for Education's workload review group on planning and resources[1] identified planning a sequence of lessons as more important than writing individual lesson plans. So what leaders can do to support this aspect of the workload challenge is to stop asking for detailed daily lesson plans, if that is current practice. It is essential for leaders to have conversations with colleagues about the difference between 'lesson planning' and 'lesson plans'. The only situation where daily lesson plans might be an expectation is when senior leaders are supporting a colleague via coaching. Here, precise planning might be needed to improve practice, in which case the plans should be prepared jointly with the senior leader as coach, as part of the larger scheme of work.

The most compelling reason for moving away from compulsory daily lesson plans is that not only are they not necessary, but they can get in the way of the bigger 'flow' of the sequence of learning. As leaders, this might appear risky. So, let's be clear about why it might not be risky to do away with daily lesson plans. First of all, what do lesson plans tell senior leaders that they don't already know? If they have an overview and indeed have had some input into some of the longer-term plans, they do not need a detailed lesson plan to tell them this. If they are honest, how many leaders read the individual lesson plans from every teacher? In a school with ten teachers and five lessons a day, that would be about 250 plans to check; with 100 teachers, 2,500 to check. Each week. Are any senior leaders doing this, seriously? And if they are, wouldn't the time be better spent going in to the actual lessons to see how things are going? Not as lesson observations, or learning walks, but simply by walking about. And offering support if needed and affirmation for work well done. How much more powerful than reading all those plans, which often bear little relation to what is happening in the classroom.

Second, senior leaders might deem it too risky to do away with lesson plans because they believe that they might be needed for an inspection. Ofsted has made it clear that they do not expect to see lesson plans, only evidence of planning. This has been made clear in its guidance document, *Ofsted inspection: myths.*[2] Apart from anything else, time is so tight on an

---

1   www.gov.uk/government/groups/teacher-workload-planning-and-resources-review-group

2   www.gov.uk/government/publications/school-inspection-handbook-from-september-2015/ofsted-inspections-mythbusting

inspection that there wouldn't be time to read files of lesson plans. The only thing which inspections comment on is impact – the impact of the delivery of curriculum plans on children's learning. It would be technically possible to have perfect plans, which do not translate into meaningful practice for children in the classroom. And the danger of this is that it is possible to be seduced into thinking that the piece of paper is the work, when in fact it is the action in the classroom.

Third, senior leaders might believe it is risky to stop insisting on lesson plans as they will have less control and view of quality assurance. But this is like a restaurant checking that all the orders have been placed so that dishes can be prepared. It suggests that the paperwork is more important than the meals that eventually end up in the restaurant. Any decent restaurant will check on the final product and tweak it to make it better, rather than thinking that the process stops at the ordering. So, for those leaders reluctant to let go of the safety net of lesson plans, they might want to trial it for half a term, then check what difference it makes not having them. Those schools which have done this have found that the quality of teaching and learning in the classroom goes up, not down. It is a case of fewer things done in greater depth.

Given the above, one of the recommendations in the 'Report of the Independent Teacher Workload Review' is that 'senior leaders should consider the cost benefit of creating larger blocks of time for this practice to make the planning activity as productive as possible and reduce the amount of time spent by individual teachers on individual planning.' As John Hattie says, 'planning can be done in many ways, but the most powerful is when teachers work together to develop plans, develop common understandings of what is worth teaching, collaborate on understanding their beliefs of challenge and progress, and work together to evaluate the impact of their planning on student outcome.'[3]

---

3   www.gov.uk/government/publications/reducing-teacher-workload-planning-and-resources-group-report

Curriculum products

'I might have taught it, but have they got it?'

There is a joke about two men in a bar. One says to his friend, 'I've taught my dog to speak French.' 'Really?' says his mate, 'let's hear him then.' 'I said I taught him, I didn't say he'd learnt it' comes the response. There is something important in this anecdote and it is this: the fact that I have taught something does not mean that my pupils have 'got' it. And they are unlikely to have really learnt something unless they produce something worthwhile with the material they are studying.

In the video explaining the rationale for the National Curriculum, Tim Oates talks about curriculum 'products'.[1] When he talks about products he means the things which pupils write, say or draw, the low stakes tests they complete or the things they make. All these provide insights for the teacher into the extent to which pupils know, understand and can do something on their own terms.

First, let's consider writing. In many parts of the sector, there is a temptation to get through the writing as fast as possible. A written piece of work requires considerable background knowledge, discussion of that knowledge and rehearsal in order for it to come together. Too

---

1   www.youtube.com/watch?v=-q5vrBXFpm0

often, pupils are set off on a writing task without sufficient 'food'. By food, I mean the stimulus, exposure to and discussion of vocabulary, use of spelling, punctuation and grammar to support meaning and modelling by the teacher. English teacher Matthew Pinkett has quite rightly said, 'Showing kids a pre-prepared model answer and asking them to write a paragraph off the back of it is no different from showing them a picture of Duck l'Orange and sending 'em to the kitchen to knock one up. Teachers must get in the habit of live modelling whenever it is required.'[2]

Writing is slow and it is difficult. But when pupils are supported and guided through the writing process carefully, the product of writing is likely to reflect what they really understand.

So we need to move away from the temptation for children to complete work which might not be original to them, such as completing closed questions on a worksheet, for example, and to conclude that they have understood, just because they have completed it. Completion of a task and understanding are not the same thing, but they are often confused. So a child is praised for having finished, before it has been checked whether they have understood it or not.

Next, let's move on to what children say. It is the responses pupils give which provide insight into whether they have understood something. If we are going to find this out, we have to spend time during the lessons asking children questions and listening carefully to their answers. This needs to happen more. Under the pressure of time, it is tempting to either take the first correct answer from one or two children and assume that everyone has 'got' it; or to complete some of the answers if they are struggling; or to take incomplete or partial answers and assume that they know the rest. What quite often happens is that children are praised for an incomplete answer and then the lesson moves on. This is not good, on several counts. First, the teacher's information is incomplete – in the rush to move on to the next part of the lesson, the brief incomplete response is taken to have more significance than it does; it is nothing more than an incomplete response and there is not enough information to judge whether to move on or not. The second reason it is not good enough is because we often need to rehearse and say our thoughts out loud before committing them to paper. As James Britton argued, 'writing floats on a sea of talk.'[3] So by

---

2   twitter.com/Positivteacha/status/950265654564806656
3   Britton, J. (1970) *Language and Learning*, Penguin.

shortcutting the responses we not only have incomplete information about the security of children's learning, we are also denying them the chance to practise articulating their thoughts. And the third reason why it is not good enough is because pupils have the right to have their ideas heard by others. By moving on too swiftly, we are cutting down their ability to refine their language and to deepen their understanding.

The importance of speaking is emphasised in the National Curriculum for English. We are doing our children a disservice if we do not both provide them with opportunities and also expect them to articulate their ideas. Many children come from backgrounds which are language poor. If we either expect partial answers, or don't ask them to speak out loud in full sentences, using subject specific vocabulary, then we are denying them the opportunity both to engage deeply with the material and also to perform well in the subject when it comes to exams.

In some, but not all, areas it is possible to gain an insight into children's thinking through their artwork or artefacts. If they have made a representation of a key idea from literature, or history, or science through sketching or through creating something and are able to talk about what they have produced and how it relates to the subject matter, then it follows that we can gain information about what they understand and where the gaps might be.

Many schools are now experimenting with thinking about real audiences for children's work. Much of what is asked of children in schools requires isolated knowledge and skills. While there is nothing wrong with this per se, the purpose of learning takes on a new dimension when we ask ourselves, where could this go, who else needs to know about this, are there links we could make with this knowledge with the wider community and who might be an external audience for what we have done?

These are some of the things they are doing: creating a class blog, preparing an exhibition with detailed notes for visitors, preparing samples of their work for governors, taking part in local and national competitions, linking with the local community on arts and environmental projects, younger children sharing their work with older pupils, and vice versa, asking family to come into school to see their work. Children are only able to engage with these wider audiences if they have something authentic to share, based on solid foundations of deep knowledge.

Beautiful work

'The best preparation for good work tomorrow is to do good work today.'
Elbert Hubbard

A few questions: do we provide enough opportunities for our pupils to produce beautiful work? Do they have the chance to polish and refine something? Are they clear about what good work looks like? Have they been inspired by the finished work of others? How often do pupils get the chance to produce work for a real audience? Are there opportunities for multiple drafts, punctuated with honest and specific feedback? The schools which do this are providing their pupils with something important – authentic work of high quality, something that pupils can be proud of.

Again, how often do pupils have access to the highest quality materials for their final work? In a Reception class in a school in Birmingham, I noticed that children were using artist-quality pastels. What was the rationale behind this? The response was interesting: if we want our pupils to produce beautiful work, we need to make sure they have the best materials. They know that these are used by professional artists. This means they take care of them, do not waste them and are inspired to do their best work. And the expense? Well, we'd rather have fewer things of the highest quality...

The notion of 'beautiful work' has been championed by Ron Berger,[1] who argues that it is possible both to meet standards and create authentic work. Underpinning this is the idea that children's work should be honoured. It should be of the highest quality and it should also have an audience. 'Once a pupil creates work of value for an authentic audience beyond the classroom – work that is sophisticated, accurate, important and beautiful – that student is never the same. When you have done quality work, deeper work, you know you are always capable of doing more.'[2]

The beautiful work exemplified by Austin's butterfly[3] did not happen overnight. Underpinning beautiful work is the imperative to draft, take feedback which is precise, robust and kind, redraft and repeat. Then we are ready to showcase to the world. The key takeaway from Austin's butterfly has been focused on the drafting and the quality of the final piece. However, it is also worth noting that this work was for a purpose: for many years, pupils in this school studied birds, and created beautiful note cards with a scientific illustration of a bird on the front and information about the bird on the back. Those cards were printed on quality card, bundled in boxed sets and sold in the community and throughout the state, including at state rest stops on highways; all the profits were used to support preservation of bird habitats.[4] And so we have the criteria here which are twofold: quality work and a real audience.

There are samples of high-quality work collected on the Models of Excellence site.[5] One, for example, where pupils aged 13-14 created a book for younger pupils, featuring original fables and accompanied by cut-block print illustrations.[6] The students studied the genre of fables, wrote personal narratives to surface issues in their own lives and created animal protagonists and stories to embed those issues in fables with helpful morals. This involved considerable practice, as they only had one chance to compose the woodcut. What is important about this is that pupils were producing both high-quality literary and artistic work. The

1   modelsofexcellence.eleducation.org/resources/illuminating-standards-video-series
2   www.edutopia.org/blog/deeper-learning-student-work-ron-berger
3   vimeo.com/159082211
4   modelsofexcellence.eleducation.org/projects/austins-butterfly-drafts
5   modelsofexcellence.eleducation.org/resources/models-excellence-ron-berger-explores-what-standards-really-look
6   modelsofexcellence.eleducation.org/resources/wolf-would-forgive-illuminating-standards-video

rules and criteria for each discipline were adhered to. This, and other examples, show how academic standards can be reached from work that is deeply artistic and connects the heart to learning.

If we want to produce more beautiful work, should we think more about the quality and quantity of worksheets, most of which do little to promote beautiful work, or should we be investing instead in high-quality sketchbooks, for example? While these are designed for art, they also make great resources for showcasing beautiful work. Work that is original, that represents the fruits of considerable labour and which are worth keeping. How much of pupils' work gets thrown away at the end of an academic year? What does this say about the sector's attitude to learning? And if funds are tight, there are electronic tools for capturing beautiful work, such as Book Creator[1] and Explain Everything.[2]

This is not to make the case that every lesson needs to produce a final produce of beautiful work. Rather it is the opposite: that there should be opportunities across the curriculum for this quality to take place, over time. It is a worthwhile endeavour not just for pupils, but for adults as well. It shifts the landscape, it raises the game and it means that we have to continually ask, is this the best it can be? It's a question worth asking: What do standards actually look like when met with integrity, depth, and imagination?

---

1   bookcreator.com
2   explaineverything.com

Curriculum pace

'The slow philosophy is not about doing everything in tortoise mode. It's less about the speed and more about investing the right amount of time and attention in the problem so you solve it.'

Carl Honoré

'Curricular materials in high-performing nations focus on fewer topics, but also communicate the expectation that those topics will be taught in a deeper, more profound way...' (Schmidt & Prawat).[1] If we are to do justice to the curriculum, we need to take the right amount of time. The pressure to rush through the material was one of the drawbacks of the previous version – it encouraged speed at the expense of depth, swiftness of coverage over security of that coverage and superficial knowledge at the expense of deep understanding. It is fair to say that the latest curriculum is more demanding and that the orders for English and maths expect children to have mastered aspects from an earlier age than they had previously. However, for all other subjects, apart from history, the content coverage is much less. Somehow,

---

1   Schmidt, W. & Prawat, R. (2006) 'Curriculum Coherence and national control of education: issue or non-issue?' *Journal of Curriculum Studies*, 38 (6) pp. 641-658

however we have got it into our heads that fast is good and slow is bad.

There was a time when some schools were encouraged to inject more pace into lessons and that was because the thread of the lesson was drifting, and, in some cases, it was sluggish, with too little being expected of pupils. However, most of that has been eradicated and instead speed trumps more thoughtful ways through the curriculum. One way of thinking about this is by considering the curriculum as a banquet. In this analogy, the gifts of the subjects are offered and opened up to children. But because speed is the trump card, they do not have enough time to do more than taste a few elements and if they do swallow some of it, they get indigestion because they are being moved quickly on to the next 'course'. If we are to honour the curriculum and children's learning, we need to think of pace differently – pace needs to be appropriate to the learning. There will be times when it is appropriate to move on quickly, but only because it is clear that the children have got it and now need something additional. Mostly, however, things need to slow down. It is simply not possible to work through a curriculum at break-neck speed. All that happens is that the destination is reached, but without any of the necessary equipment or indicators to be able to say whether it had been a successful journey or not.

When pace is privileged over security of content, there is often some confusion between the work and the learning and it goes something like this: well, we have done it, so they should have got it. But between the doing and the being able to say that they have got it, lessons need to slow down so that the curriculum matter can be properly digested. And this can only be done through talk, discussion, making mistakes and addressing misconceptions. Mistakes need to be celebrated as the launchpad for new learning – if all our pupils understand things the first time round then the work is probably too easy. And the demands of the new curriculum, which require greater depth, mean that it is no longer reasonable or realistic to plough on at great speed.

What are we doing when we slow down? We are not talking here about going at a snail's pace, but at the appropriate pace for deep learning. When we get this right, we are allowing pupils to engage with material – this should be source material wherever possible, either extracts or full texts, according to the ages of the pupils – to go through unfamiliar words, talk about them in context, check for pupils' understanding of these terms and ask them to make sense of the material.

In fact, in everything we do, we should be getting to the heart of the matter.

And it is the appropriate use of pace which allows us to help our pupils to go deeper and learn better. To really take this to heart and put it into practice, it means that we do not take superficial, one-word answers, but expect pupils to explain their reasons, to listen carefully to their responses and to expect other pupils to do so, and ask them whether they agree or not. If we are helping our children to infer as well as to take on board surface details, we need to probe, to check what they are thinking and to see if their peers agree. One way to make this more efficient is to ask the pupils to talk in pairs about what they understand the key points to be. While this is happening, it is possible to wander round the room, listening to what they say. Then, when it is time to bring things together, it is possible to highlight some of the things which have been heard: 'I noticed that you focused on this, can you tell us why? What do the rest of you think?' and 'Over here, I'm not sure that you understood the question correctly. What do you think it means? Do the rest of you agree?'

By slowing down and going deeper, we not only make things more meaningful for children, we are also able to select fewer resources, which we explore in depth, rather than racing through a pile of irrelevant material.

Developing expertise

'True intuitive expertise is learned from prolonged experience with good feedback on mistakes.'
Daniel Kahneman

If we are serious about the curriculum, we need to think about how pupils develop expertise. There is a paradox to this and it links to mastery – if we are expert at something or have mastered something, the conundrum is that we realise how much there still is to know and understand. At its heart, expertise is knowing something really well; the nuts and bolts and are able to show this in different contexts.

This will look different for different age groups, but underpinning expertise will be pupils' ability to describe the key elements of what they have learnt, in their own words, and to show how this can be applied in different contexts. A child in Key Stage 1 will be an expert in story-telling if they are creating stories using their own ideas, with correct spellings, punctuation and grammar. It will be recognisably individual to them, rather than something which has been heavily scaffolded and similar to every other piece of work in the class. This doesn't happen overnight, and scaffolding will need to be in place at the early stages, but these should be removed as soon as possible so that the child's own unique take on the subject can emerge.

If every child in the class is producing work which is remarkably similar and if they are not able to articulate what they have learnt in their own words and in their writing, then it is unlikely that they have developed in that topic. They are likely to be parroting back what the teacher has said and completing identical worksheets or closed writing frames, which mask the limitation of what they know. At a superficial glance, it might appear that they have 'got it', but a brief conversation with them will reveal whether this is the case or not. And quite often it isn't. Too many children, when asked what they are doing in a lesson and why they are doing it, are not sure. Their eyes swivel back to the board and the learning objectives, which they repeat back, word for word. When this happens and they are not able to describe what they are doing and why, in their own words, they are not in the process of developing expertise.

Developing expertise is messy. Not every child will do it the same way. The unique products, namely what children say and write, are the ways in which teachers find out whether they have really understood. This applies whether it is the basic nuts and bolts of spelling, punctuation and grammar or explaining their working-out in maths, writing an account of rainforests in geography or a piece of creative writing in English. The difference between superficial and deep learning is an important one; it can appear as though a child has produced a lot of work, but it is possible that they are completing the tasks set rather than being shown how they can be deeply learnt.

The route to deep learning and expertise is, to quote Tim Oates, fewer things in greater depth.[1] When the curriculum is offered in this way, without an overload of props and activities, we have the chance to get to deep learning and the development of expertise. When we produce too many resources or plan too many activities, these can become proxies for learning. It is possible to be convinced that learning has taken place because so much has happened. In fact, what has really happened is that plenty of activities have taken place and without the slower, tentative conversations about what the heart of the matter really is, this can create a false impression of busyness masquerading as learning. The text, the source

---

1   www.cambridgeassessment.org.uk/insights/national-curriculum-tim-oates-on-assessment-insights

material, the scientific artefacts and the maths should have the limelight. It is tempting to dumb things down, to make them easy and accessible, but if every child is entitled to a rich and demanding curriculum, they need to be provided with and guided through the hard stuff.

If everything is easy, it is hard for learning to take place. Expertise comes through the struggle of not knowing everything, having sufficient support and making sense of it on our own terms. This is not about letting children flounder, it is rather about providing them with high-quality material and supporting them to get to grips with it and apply it in new settings. When starting something new, scaffolding needs to be there so that unnecessary time isn't wasted, but if that scaffolding remains too long, it prevents deep learning and expertise from taking place. This is because it is easy to become reliant on the structures rather than dealing with the discomfort which comes from having a go and not getting it.

The second condition which needs to be in place is sufficient time. When something complicated is expected to be covered in one or two lessons, it is very unlikely that expertise can be developed. Without the longer periods, over time, it is unlikely that the deep, intellectual architecture can be developed. This deep space is like a bucket which holds the big ideas of the aspect of the curriculum which is being learnt. If this is done properly, it means that new knowledge can be added quickly. Without the deep work, the new knowledge floats around without any organising structure to it. So what might seem time-consuming at the start is actually an investment in time, so that when more detail and knowledge is added, it links to existing earlier knowledge, which is held together in the deep structure. For example, if we have paid enough attention to helping children understand new material, when they come to see new data and information about the subject, they are able to make sense of it and discuss it in the new context, because the connections have already been made.

Section 3: Assessment and Feedback

Assessment

'Assessment is, indeed, the bridge between teaching and learning.'
Dylan Wiliam

The word 'assessment' comes from the Latin 'to sit alongside'. Now, it is not realistic for us to sit alongside every pupil. But it does have something to tell us about how we might think about assessment – that it is the process of gaining insight into what our pupils know, understand and can do as a result of what we have taught them. In doing this, we will have greater insight into what appears to have been learnt, what needs to be consolidated or revisited and where the gaps are.

If the purpose of robust curriculum planning is to ensure that pupils are taught the demanding aspects of a topic, then checking whether they have got it needs to be done through assessment. There are formal and informal ways of doing this. Not all results of assessment instruments need to be captured on spreadsheets or other documents. But whether documented formally or not, the information should be fine-tuning the next stages in learning.

At its lightest touch, assessment can be done through talk. In fact, I would argue that assessment for learning involves high-quality conversations about learning and then acting on that information. Dylan Wiliam, whose work was instrumental in driving assessment for learning in schools, said 'responsive teaching' is one side of the coin: I have taught something and I need to know whether my pupils have 'got it' and to what depth? The information I gain from this light-touch assessment will determine where the learning and the work go next. It is through the 'to and fro' of questioning conversations in the classroom that I know not only whether pupils have completed something, but whether they have understood and are able to apply it in different contexts. There are very effective ways of developing this across a class – the work done by Alex Quigley[1] on techniques such as A, B, and C. The teacher asks a question, one pupil gives an answer (A) a second pupil builds on it (B) and a third either contradicts or contributes (C). Building this kind of structure during lessons, with no hands up, so that any child, within reason,[2] can be asked a question without warning, ensures that all are kept on their toes, and have to listen to one another's answers in order to be able to contribute. If, as a result of doing something like this, I find that pupils are able to respond with A and B but have less to either contradict or make further contributions, then I will realise that there is more to do. Conversely, if all seem secure, then I will make the decision to move on. The second side of the assessment for learning coin is this: what pupils will do differently as a result of the feedback: how will they change their work and how will I know?

If the purpose of this light-touch assessment is to provide information about where to go next, then this is formative assessment. The critical thing is that it provides information about where the gaps are and also what can be celebrated, in terms of the distance travelled – so that we and our pupils are able to say we didn't know that before and now we do. And there is still this to be grappled with and understood. Whatever information is gathered and whatever feedback is given to pupils, the important thing is that they act on it.

Too much feedback is generic and imprecise, such as 'use more imaginative vocabulary in your writing.' Well, the pupil would have used more imaginative vocabulary if they'd known that more imaginative vocabulary was available. Without the prompts for the missing links, pupils are likely to be adrift. There is more on this in the chapter on feedback and marking.

More formal, but still low stakes assessments, are also part of the assessment process. For example, pupils sit vocabulary tests, times tables

---

1   www.theconfidentteacher.com/2013/12/disciplined-discussion-easy-abc
2   Caveat here: I would not call on a pupil if I knew they had been recently bereaved, for example. But I would check that they were paying attention.

tests and key terms recall, and all provide opportunities for checking whether something has been learnt. The most powerful way, identified by Dylan Wiliam, is for the results of these sorts of tests to be private to the pupil. They need to be reassured that there is no shame in getting things wrong, because, with practice, that is how we learn. It is in the process of trying to recall an answer that the learning, in other words, what is remembered, becomes stronger. Both multiple-choice and short-answer quizzes enhance later performance.[3]

It also appears that if we get an answer incorrect, our neural pathways are more sensitive to finding the correct answer. So, the paradox is that learning is often more powerful, albeit uncomfortable, when we get things wrong and search out the correct answer, than when we get something correct in the first place. If pupils know this, they are likely to persevere longer with knowing and remembering things. A further benefit of this light-touch but efficient way of assessing is that it demands revisiting. And it is the revisiting, over time, which secures the learning in the long-term memory.

A further benefit of assessment is that it is possible to see the distance travelled. It is deeply rewarding to see the difference in knowledge and proficiency at the start of a course or unit of work, as we make progress through it and at the end. When we consider examples like Austin's Butterfly, we can see that through careful critique and feedback, those basic attempts, refined and practised over time, become solid pieces of work. It was in the assessing, discussion and reworking that the impressive piece of work was produced. This would not have been possible without thoughtful, sensitive and robust assessment.

---

3   psycnet.apa.org/doiLanding?doi=10.1037%2Fxap0000004

Curriculum without levels

'There are a number of compelling reasons for levels being dropped.'
Tim Oates

Levels have been removed from the National Curriculum. There are several reasons for this: first, they had become disconnected from their original purpose, which had been to create a system which would show progress through a curriculum. But, in spite of their good intentions, they were used for purposes for which they were never intended. They were only ever 'best fit indicators' to describe standards at the end of a key stage; they were not able to provide information about what a pupil could or could not do, they were never designed to be broken down into sub-levels or for fine measures of progress, their use often meant that pupils were rushed through content due to the cliff-edge threshold between levels, they gave a false impression of parity between subject and they implied that progress is linear. As Jamie Pembroke argues, 'progress is catching up, filling gaps, deepening understanding, and overcoming barriers. As much as we'd like it to, can all this really be accurately represented by a single, simple, linear point scale?'[1] And there were real problems when they became connected to performance management, because teachers were under pressure to 'show' progress through improving and rising scores on spreadsheets, which might often mask significant gaps in learning.

A couple of examples to exemplify this; Shaun Allison, deputy head teacher at the Durrington School: 'The first, was when I was observing somebody who came for a job interview at our school. During the lesson he said the following: "If your target is a level 5, you can try the extension task." Now, I'm sure many of us have said similar, but if we unpick that statement, it's not useful. Why should we limit deep thinking to those students who have managed to acquire the arbitrary label of a level 5? Why not seek to challenge all students to think more deeply? The second was from a headteacher, reflecting on the presentation on our approach: "Thinking about it, our KS3 teacher assessments are always bang on target or above... but our GCSE results are awful!" This speaks for itself. Levels haven't really provided us with accurate assessment information.'[2]

The removal of levels in the latest curriculum allows schools to move to a model based on focused assessment of the specifics of the curriculum. As chair of the expert panel that reviewed the National Curriculum between 2010 and 2013, Tim Oates studied many high performing jurisdictions across the world and found a common theme among them was that primary school age children studied fewer things in greater depth. 'They secured deep learning in central concepts and ideas. Assessment should focus on whether children have understood these key concepts rather than achieved a particular level.'[3] There continues however, to be a problem, particularly at Key Stage 3, where assessments are linked to the criteria for GCSE. These statements were only ever intended to be used as descriptors for the final exam, they were never meant to be criteria for judging work in earlier key stages. What seems to have happened is that in attempting to prepare younger pupils for the demands of the GCSE, there has been undue focus on the generic skills, rather than concentrating on the content to be learnt for that key stage. As Daisy Christodoulu says, 'Curriculum planning and its formative assessment should be structured

---

1   sigplus.blogspot.co.uk/2016/04/5-golden-rules-of-tracking.html
2   classteaching.wordpress.com/2015/02/12/assessment-without-levels-the-story-so-far
3   www.cambridgeassessment.org.uk/insights/national-curriculum-tim-oates-on-assessment-insights

around mastery of the building blocks, not 'retrofitted' to the test structure and requirements.'[4]

So, the new curriculum provides far more specific age-related content with an increased expectation of attainment. The question in relation to assessment is simple: if I have taught it, have they got it? And if not, how do I know? And it is here that questions are helpful. For example, with multiple choice questions, pupils will identify the correct answer or answers if they truly understand the distinctions in the range of possible answers. Daisy Christodoulou has some helpful examples[5] which show the power of thoughtful questions. In one version: which of the following words can be used as a verb?

    a) run

    b) tree

    c) car

    d) person

    e) apple

It is likely that the majority of pupils will get the correct answer. However, a more nuanced response to pupils' understanding is likely to emerge from a question such as:

In which sentences is 'cook' a verb?

    a) I cook a meal.

    b) He is a good cook.

    c) The cook prepared a nice meal.

    d) Every morning, they cook breakfast.

    e) That restaurant has a great cook.

And it is in the discussion about the correct answers which both support the identification of misconceptions and secure deeper learning. It is the use of these which provides clearer insights into what pupils really understand.

The second area which needs to be considered relates to comparative judgement.[6] Instead of the artificiality of vague criteria, we look at pupils' work and make judgements about which is better. This calls on the innate professional knowledge of teachers and, when carried out at scale, across a school or nationally, it provides a greater degree of reliability and locates

---

4   Christodoulou, D. (2017) *Making Good Progress*, Oxford University Press.

5   thewingtoheaven.wordpress.com/2015/06/07/assessment-alternatives-1-using-questions-instead-of-criteria

6   www.nomoremarking.com

the quality in the actual work itself. The work on comparative judgement is still being developed and it might not be suitable for every part of the curriculum. The greatest benefit is that it gets teachers talking about the features of quality work and how these might be developed in their own classrooms. Jen Reynolds, a teacher and adviser, has written about how she has worked with local schools to make judgements about the quality of pupils' written work. There are a number of promising aspects to the comparative judgement work – teachers reading lots of work by children from other schools, being able to see how the work of their own classes compares with others, a clear picture of what strong work looks like and what gaps might need to be addressed, and a real sense of professional collaboration rather than suspicion and defensiveness, which sometimes characterises moderation sessions. Comparative judgement meets the criteria for a curriculum without levels.

And in thinking about the curriculum without levels, we need to remember this, from Tim Oates' work: levels reinforced dysfunctional ideas about individual ability. In contrast, high achieving schools and systems use a Confucian assumption: 'every child is capable of learning anything, depending on the way it is presented to them and the effort they put into learning it'.[7] From this it can be seen that the removal of 'levels' was not some arbitrary change in bureaucracy, but a fundamental shift in thinking about both assessment and learning.

---

7   www.youtube.com/watch?v=-q5vrBXFpm0

Feedback and marking

'The first fundamental principle of effective classroom feedback is that feedback should be more work for the recipient than the donor.'

Dylan Wiliam

High-quality feedback has always been fundamental to supporting pupil progress. However, it appears that marking has become a proxy for feedback and this has become a significant pressure point for teachers. The question needs to be asked, 'Who is this for?' The pressure to produce large amounts of written marking means that it is often done quickly, comments are superficial and 'next steps' are vague. Often, pupils are not sure how to improve their work because feedback such as 'use more technical vocabulary' is not exemplified. This means that pupils are likely to be confused about what they should include.

The problem with the focus on written feedback is that it appears to have trumped high-quality verbal feedback during lessons. While there might have been verbal feedback, some schools worry that there is no hard evidence that it has taken place. And as a result, teachers often resort to verbal feedback stamps, to prove that they have spoken to the pupil about their work. This is a waste of time. In a desperate effort to prove that pupils are making progress, the marks and stamps in books and photos of practical work are used as devices to show others, not necessarily the children, that feedback has been given. The problem here is that the written feedback and the sundry stamps are often taken as proxies for progress. But they do not show that pupils have made progress, they only show that someone has made some marks on the paper.

However, feedback is important because it shifts the learning on, as long as pupils do something effective with the feedback. The question is, does it need to be written every time and how can progress be shown if not?

The most effective way to consider progress is to look at pupils' work and have discussions with them, over time. Have they improved over the last few weeks? Is there a direction of improvement? Is their work showing higher levels of nuanced language and understanding of the concepts and detail being taught? Are they getting better results in low stakes quizzes on the essentials they need to know? Are they able to talk about what they know, understand and can do? These are authentic ways of checking progress, because they reside in the products and speech of pupils.

A further problem with trying to prove progress is that it assumes that learning happens in a linear fashion. We know that it doesn't. In fact, we often need to forget things, revisit them, get things wrong, correct them, for deep learning to take place. This happens when there is high-quality discussion about what makes good work and pupils have the chance to draft, and if necessary, redraft their work. So, while it is not necessary to check every piece of work, every day, it is possible to skim books and to pull out the key points which a number of pupils are still getting wrong. These misconceptions and mistakes are the platform for new learning, as the teacher revisits these at the start of the next lesson. A quick note on a grid will highlight those areas which are secure and a cause for celebration, and those where there are gaps, which need to be revisited. Not only does this save time, it is more effective in terms of moving learning on, of providing honest feedback and securing deeper progress, over time.

Excessive focus on marking books mean that other things do not get done. Things that make a difference to learning, such as planning. So, what can be done to square the circle? First, let's ask who the marking is for. If it is for accountability to senior leaders and inspectors, then the question is why? Ofsted has produced clarification on expectations here. It makes it clear that Ofsted does not expect to see a particular frequency or quantity of work in pupils' books or folders. Nor does it expect to see unnecessary or extensive written dialogue between teachers and pupils in exercise books and folders. Ofsted recognises the importance of different forms of feedback and inspectors will look at how these are used to promote learning.

There are three references to marking in the Ofsted Inspection Handbook.[1] The first reference places marking in the context of what constitutes teaching, the second in terms of evaluating learning over time and the third is in the criteria for outstanding quality of teaching. It might be helpful to consider the second two references to marking and think through implications for schools. Para 183, 'Evaluating learning over time', says that direct observation of lessons needs to be supplemented by other evidence to enable inspectors to evaluate what teaching is like typically and the impact that teaching has had on pupils' learning over time. So this additional information includes: the school's own evaluations of the quality of teaching and its impact on learning, discussions with pupils about the work they have undertaken, what they have learned from it and their experience of teaching and learning over longer periods, discussion about teaching and learning with teachers, teaching assistants and other staff and the views of pupils, parents and staff. Also a scrutiny of pupils' work, with particular attention to whether marking, assessment and testing are carried out in line with the school's policy and whether they are used effectively to help teachers improve pupils' learning. There is also a focus on the level of challenge provided, and whether pupils have to grapple appropriately with content, not necessarily 'getting it right' first time, which could be evidence that the work is too easy. And finally looking at pupils' effort and success in completing their work and the progress they make over a period of time.

---

1   www.gov.uk/government/publications/school-inspection-handbook-from-september-2015

So there's a raft of evidence to consider. Why, then, the focus on volumes of marking? It's much healthier to think of marking as feedback which supports progress over time. Evidence of progress over time is much more powerful than over-marking, which goes nowhere. Sensible feedback and marking policies state clearly what the purpose and rationale for these are; they recognise that one size does not fit every subject or key stage and encourage colleagues to think creatively about gathering evidence of progress. There are some schools that are thinking hard about the impact of marking. Andrew Percival has written about his school's approach to marking.[2] Drawing on the research[3] on marking, he and his colleagues asked themselves whether the quality of the feedback was as good as it could be; whether the pupils were taking responsibility for their own learning and whether the pressures of marking meant that teachers did not have time to do other, more worthwhile activities. These are important questions which everyone in school should be asking. They removed the expectation for written comments in books. However, the books are checked quickly and common strengths, mistakes and misconceptions are shared with the whole class at the start of the next lesson. First, this has far greater impact and second, it saves teachers' time.

And the logical extension to this is comparative judgement.

2   primarypercival.weebly.com/blog/no-written-marking-job-done
3   A summary of the research on marking by Adam Boxer: achemicalorthodoxy.
     wordpress.com/2018/02/18/markaggedon/#more-2134

On filling the gaps

'The doorstep to the temple of wisdom is a knowledge of our own ignorance.'

Benjamin Franklin

Richard Feynman, Nobel physicist and creator of the Feynman lectures and books, kept notebooks. When Feynman was due to take his oral examinations after his second year at Princeton, he set aside some time to prepare. He opened a notebook and wrote down all the things that he still didn't know and worked on these.

In one response to Cal Newport's article,[4] a student described how he used this technique. He would write out something (in this example, the process of digestion) and put a query or question mark against the elements he wasn't sure about. These were the areas for him to go back and revisit. When we just think about the things we already know, this only takes us so far. We also need to pay attention to the things we don't know or where our knowledge is shaky.

Now, I think that there could be something really powerful here about using the Feynman notebook method to consolidate learning, secure mastery, fill the gaps and show progress. With the new focus on the wider

---

4   calnewport.com/blog/2015/11/25/the-feynman-notebook-method

curriculum beyond English, maths and science in primary, what would happen if every child had a 'things I don't know' notebook? As they work through the wider subjects in the curriculum, they write down the things they know and have found out on one page, then ask questions about things they still don't know about on the opposite page. It is important to leave lines and plenty of space so that these can either be filled in or referenced at a later date.

This would fulfil a number of important elements in securing a robust curriculum: it would provide clear evidence to the pupil of the trajectory of their learning – there would be visible evidence of the amount they knew at the beginning and how much they knew by the end of the unit. This is highly motivating. The questions are important because they identify where the knowledge is insecure, or they identify what else they would like to know (which is exactly what Feynman did). Furthermore, these questions provide a route map for both what needs to be learnt in the short term, and bigger questions which can be left for the pupil to think about and research in due course.

An important element of securing deep learning is the revisiting of key concepts and adding new information which links and connects to prior schemata. The notebook method is a visible and concrete way of making this happen.

From the teacher's point of view, this would provide clear evidence both for their own planning and also for showing progress of learning over time. One notebook could last for the year and would provide a rich source of concrete knowledge about what has been learnt, where the gaps have been and where these have been later filled. And also, what still needs to be learnt. Because the paradox of mastery is that once we are in a place of deep knowledge, we realise how little we know and how much more there is to find out.

In terms of contrasting this with much common practice in subjects beyond English, maths and science, where the learning is frequently documented through worksheets, which too often put limits on learning, mostly these are used as evidence that something has been learnt, when in fact, all that has really occurred is that the pupil has completed the sheet. It makes no further demands on their cognitive development, requires no self-reflection and provides the shallowest proxies for learning. The authenticity and messiness of the notebook method is in stark contrast to this. It is an honest reflection of what a pupil knows and what they know they still have to do.

Differentiation

'Of all the impossible tasks expected of poor, overworked teachers, differentiation is one of the most troublesome.'
David Didau

There has been a ton of time wasted on differentiation. It is very important to keep teacher practices under review so that there is an absolute focus on the impact on learning. These are the reasons why differentiation doesn't usually work:

First, differentiation anticipates what children are capable of – by giving them prepared worksheets according to their ability, we are limiting what they might be capable of, because the work usually puts a cap on what they can do.

Second, the materials prepared for differentiation are usually closed exercises. So all that children have to do is complete these. Completion of prepared materials does not allow them to interrogate the material, struggle with it and make sense of it on their own terms. This applies to all those with materials differentiated in advance.

Third, it cuts down on the possibility of addressing misconceptions. Because the materials have been prepared in advance so that the children can complete them, they usually have less cognitive challenge in them. Cognitive challenge is at the heart of learning – if a child does not have the chance to struggle with demanding material, they are not really gaining new knowledge and skills.

Fourth, the completion of the worksheet is often regarded as the work. Children finish something and are praised for it, without checking for sure that they have properly understood. It is too easy to complete work which has been prepared in advance by guessing, prompting or copying from someone else. This places very little demand on them, but has the superficial attraction of making them appear busy. Busy is not the point- learning is.

Finally, they create a lot of extra work for teachers. Extra work is fine if it results in better outcomes, but it is a waste of time when it doesn't.

Above all, differentiation goes against the heart of the principles of the new curriculum, which is that all children should be following the same course of work, are entitled to do difficult things and are supported on the way. So what is the difference between support and differentiation? Well, support consists of the live conversations and additional unpacking of the material during the lesson. Differentiating materials in advance predetermines what children are able to do.

This places different demands on the teacher. Instead of staying up half the night to prepare different coloured resources for the different groups of children, they get a decent night's sleep. They have time for family and friends rather than slaving over resources. Instead, they use the text or the problem or the big idea as their starting point for the lesson. All children are entitled to the richness and difficulty of authentic material. Teachers talk about it and then ask children to engage with the material, whether it is inferring some important aspects, which might not be immediately apparent, and ask them to show what they know and can do with the material. The expectation is that all children will work on this. And the support comes through live conversations with those who haven't grasped it or who are struggling. It expects children to do more with less. And it expects children to think and to do something with it on their own terms. This is light years away from completing a prepared sheet.

A very good example of this happened in a maths lesson. What is interesting about this is that the pupils were told, 'This is a beautiful problem' – note the way that the teacher describes their work as 'beautiful'. He is signposting that this is intriguing, elegant and worthwhile. In talking through with the pupils how to work out a complicated angle between two polygons, he carefully goes through with them how to work out the angles, pausing to take answers from them. All are listening, concentrating and contributing. It becomes clear that one pupil is not sure how to combine two angles to arrive at the answer. The teacher quickly opens another page on the board and goes through a simpler example, asking her to tell him what the steps are. Then he returns to the main problem and she is able to see what to do. Now, what is interesting about this is that the whole group benefited from this additional exercise in working out the angles. It was an efficient way of both addressing one pupil's misconception and reinforcing the procedure for the rest of the group. There was a sigh of pleasure from the class when the pupil realised what to do. There is no way that this could have been achieved through a pre-prepared worksheet. Her misconception would have gone unnoticed until the work was taken in. The feedback was live and both the individual and the group benefited.

There are similar examples where the teacher has realised that pupils did not understand the meaning of 'infer'. Although this had been discussed and checked, it was apparent as she went round the class, as they were inferring what the writer intended, that they were not going deep enough, but only gathering surface information. Again, the class was stopped so that they could go through the difference between surface information, which is important but only takes us so far, and the deeper meaning implied by the writer. This gave a chance for contributions from those who were more secure, providing an opportunity for them to consolidate their work on inference, and supported those who were not clear about how to read a text more deeply. Again, there was no way that this could have been anticipated in advance and any pre-prepared worksheets would have masked the fact that some pupils would struggle with this.

As David Didau argues in 'What do teachers think differentiation is?', 'All that's required is that teachers are flexible and skilled enough to be able to veer off-piste to collect up confused students as and when required. So, death to the tyrannical old approaches to differentiation and viva adaptive instruction!'[1]

---

1   www.learningspy.co.uk/research/teachers-think-differentiation

Challenge

'Accept the challenges so that you can feel the exhilaration of victory.'
George S. Patton

We all know someone who spends some of their downtime working on a crossword, doing a sudoku, a puzzle, or a word search. Why are we spending money and time on activities which are essentially tests? Businesses are making large profits out of the fact that we like testing ourselves. What is that about? Well, is it because we enjoy the deep satisfaction of struggling with something, thinking hard about it, getting it wrong, going back and correcting it, realising our mistake and then getting the right solution? Critical to this is that it is done in private. No one is watching, no one is making us feel like a muppet. We get cross with ourselves, but that's different. There is no one out there pointing at us and making us feel inadequate. The struggle and the joy are personal private things.

We can make the case from this that we are a challenge-seeking species; we like doing things that are difficult, as long as the conditions are right. This means that when we make mistakes, these are seen as opportunities for learning, rather than shame. Furthermore, there is evidence that regular, low stakes testing secures knowledge in the long-term memory.[2]

---

2   physics.creodont.co.uk/afl-feedback-and-the-low-stakes-testing-effect

This is because the active effort in recalling the information results in longer-term security of that information.

And what do pupils have to say about challenge? Alison Peacock, in 'Assessment for Learning without Limits',[1] provides an insight into children's views on challenge: 'The 'more able' loved it; they enjoyed being the 'bright' ones and having 'special' challenges set by the teacher. The middle group were annoyed that they didn't get the same work and challenges as the other group; they wanted to try harder work but they have worked out they would never be moved up as there were only six seats on the top table. The 'less able' were affected the most. They felt 'dumb', useless, they thought they would never be allowed challenges as they usually work with the teaching assistant – some by year 5 were completely dependent on the teaching assistant to help them. This 'less able' group liked the sound of some of the challenges the top group had, but knew they would never get the chance.'

For many of the 'lower' groups, they are offered closed responses – matching parts of sentences, filling in gaps, completing easy worksheets, none of which really stretch them or expect them to do much. Others, by contrast are given more to do and more is expected of them. While they might have a few closed exercises in order to practise or consolidate their knowledge, they are also expected to do new things with this – constructing their own sentences, coming up with alternative adjectives in a piece of writing, suggesting alternatives to maths problems. These children are being given more opportunities, both to struggle and to gain new knowledge. The others, by contrast, have insufficient work expected of them and as a result, don't make the same gains as their peers. This extends the gap in their knowledge and attainment. The paradox is that by attempting to give them easier work, such exercises can often close down their capacity and opportunity to do more.

A couple of examples from the secondary context. When a group of high prior attaining students, who were also disaffected, were asked if they were doing their best in any particular subject, they said that they tried their hardest in geography. When asked why this was the case, the students said that their teacher gave them articles to read for homework, some of which would be used by undergraduates at university. She told them to read an article and reassured them that they would not understand it all,

---

1   Peacock, A. (2016) *Assessment for Learning without limits*, Open University Press.

but that it would be discussed at the start of the next lesson, where they would unpack what they did understand and what they did not. In providing them with material that was above their pay-grade, she was giving them the message that they were capable of tackling challenging work. The subsequent discussion at the start of the next lesson meant that all students were able to access demanding material. In a later conversation relating to this account, another colleague reported that she had turned up to do a cover lesson for a Year 9 class and no work had been set. So, she taught them the Year 12 lesson, which she had done on the geo-political situation in Syria. When asked what the impact had been, she responded that the Year 9 pupils were fascinated and 'you could have heard a pin drop.' This is not to make the case that the Key Stage 3 curriculum should be based on an A level course, rather that we have plenty of headroom as a profession to raise the bar in terms of the material offered and the expectations we have of pupils. The crucial thing here is that pupils are not left to flounder – they are offered challenging material and they are supported, through talk and scaffolding. This is a contrast to differentiated worksheets, which are time-consuming to resource and prepare and which essentially dumb down the curriculum offer for some pupils.

The main takeaway from this is that pupils are keen to do difficult work. It is seen as a privilege to be thought capable of tackling demanding material. If we do not think this through and assume that challenge is only for some, then we are in danger, as Christine Counsell argues, of offering narrow narratives or by giving up on disciplinary rigour altogether for some pupils.[2] If we are serious about narrowing gaps, we cannot be serious about signing up for a different diet for pupils of varying prior attainment. Apart from those pupils with significant additional needs, we should be making the case that the material studied is demanding, challenging and that access to that material is secured through talk, modelling and practice.

This is an argument for challenge, for all. There is an odd notion in some parts of the sector that challenge is something additional, or enrichment, or something offered to bright pupils. If we go down this route, we are saying that demanding, interesting work is rationed for some, rather than being an entitlement for all.

---

2   www.tandfonline.com/doi/full/10.1080/09585176.2011.574951

Section 4:
Curriculum
Instruments

Question kleptomaniacs

'Question everything. Learn something.'
Euripides

Tim Oates has talked about the power of questions. Speaking about the new curriculum published by the Department for Education in 2013, he argued that one of the most powerful ways for teachers to open up the content of the curriculum was through questions.[1] He went so far as to say that they should become question 'kleptomaniacs'. So what is it about the garnering of questions that is worth pursuing?

First, they make us think about what it is that we want pupils to learn. Framing questions is a way of shifting focus from content coverage, to the key concepts and ideas, which we want pupils to know at a deep level. The work on long-term memory by Willingham and others should be at the heart of our thinking about curriculum planning and lesson delivery. The long-term memory is the place where connections and links are held together in schemata, or organising categories. Without the absolute focus on long-term memory, experiences in the classroom can often become a string of unrelated facts and elements, which have no holding power, or stickiness.

---

1   www.youtube.com/watch?v=-q5vrBXFpm0

The consequence of lots of material, without access to the organising structures, means that the working memory is overloaded. Finding good questions helps form the bridge between the working memory and long-term memory. To take an example – let's suppose we are teaching about commas. We want pupils to understand that grammar in general, and commas in this particular instance, help us to write fluently and to make sense to the reader. They are not there for ornaments, nor as an end in themselves, but are the servants of great literacy. In other words, both what we write and in what we read. So, the simple question here is, 'why do we use commas and full stops?' This, in turn, helps us to see what the pupils need to encounter, in order to get the purpose of using full stops and commas both in their own work and understanding how they help the flow of others' writing. The lesson then turns on the question of what happens when we don't use full stops and commas, and an example of prose without these can be shown and pupils asked whether there are any problems with the punctuation. We might then ask them, well what would help this make sense? Would a pause here help? Is there a different point being made here? And through the power of questions, pupils come to see these fundamental conventions of literacy as supporting the meaning and flow of writing, rather than as odd things which they are told to include.

This way of thinking about lesson planning supports the learning going into the long-term memory. This is because pupils see the bigger picture and purpose of what they are learning; they can make the connections from the particular to the general. And in working this way, they are being supported to build up the schemata, which can be drawn on in future. It stops the curriculum from being atomised and shifts it to a larger space where pupils can access it in future.

Questions also shift the focus onto purpose. Framing questions means that we have to think about the subject in order get to the heart of the substance. As a teacher, I need to ask myself, what is the key point here? What is the main concept that needs to be developed over time, so that pupils can make sense of the material? To take the example of teaching pupils about the commandments in Judaism; we might argue that the underlying principle of the 613 mitzvot is an expression of the Jewish covenant- the idea that abiding by these rules is a way of showing commitment to the contract of being part of the Jewish tradition. So, early work on this might involve what is meant by a covenant, what are the expectations on either side, what happens when one side does not keep to their part of the agreement. It then means that when individual commandments are considered, they are understood in the context of a deal, or agreement with God, rather than as a list of odd things to do.

Questions are a very efficient way of gaining information about what pupils understand. Tim Oates has argued that it is through the use of oral and written responses that teachers have insights into the extent to which what has been taught has been understood. He and others, including Joe Kirby, have shown the potential for multiple-choice questions.[2] While these have had a bad press over the years, they are now seen as having the potential to provide insights into learning. When they are carefully constructed, so that some answers are very close to others, they can provide nuanced information about what has been learnt.

And don't let us forget the Bloom's questions. These have also had a bad press because there has been a focus on getting to the 'higher order' questions of analysing, applying *etc* as though knowledge and understanding were less important. As Tom Sherrington has argued, the opposite is the case.[3] We cannot analyse without knowing stuff, so the core work has to be on the knowledge. The rest flows from that. It is more helpful to think of the Bloom's questions as a range of questions, rather than as a taxonomy. When we do that, we have very powerful tools to open up the learning, to make greater cognitive demands on pupils. And we are able to do this without preparing masses of additional resources. The questions themselves are the resource. To take an example; 'Goldilocks and the Three Bears'. I need to know that my pupils know the story and can recount it in their own words. When using a range of questions – such as, what would happen if Goldilocks came to your home, which bit of the story did you like best, can you think of a different ending to the story? – as teachers, we gain further insights into how well they have understood the original material. Furthermore, the range of questions will place differing cognitive loads on them, so that from simple material comes the subtlety of deep engagement with the material.

Finally, questions are very efficient, because they don't take up masses of physical resources or worksheets.

---

2   pragmaticreform.wordpress.com/2014/03/08/whymcqs
3   teacherhead.com/2018/03/19/evidence-informed-ideas-every-teacher-should-know-about

Mastery

'One of the odd things about being a writer is that you never reach a point of certainty, a point of mastery where you can say, "Right. Now I understand how this is done."'
Jenny Offill

Mastery has entered educational discourse in the last few years. And the paradox in the quote above is that when we reach a place of mastery we realise how little we know, how much more there is to do. But it is, however, an exciting place to be. The problem is that too much of pupils' work is over-scaffolded, overladen with writing strips and generally over-supported. A further problem is that a race through the curriculum means that the material is atomised and the pupil never gets the chance to see how their work sits within a bigger picture.

Planning for mastery needs to be over time, not a one-lesson objective. A good example of this is some work done by the Swiss Cottage School. To elucidate this way of thinking about the curriculum, the school created 'The allegory of the guitar' as a way of discussing different approaches to planning and progress. In this example, two pupils, who were volunteers, had the learning intention to 'learn to play the guitar in front of a live audience'. What is interesting about this, is that there is an ambitious goal and an authentic purpose. However, to achieve it will require practice, spaced learning, learning from mistakes and acting on feedback. It also means that there will be times when the pupil is discouraged, goes backwards, gets frustrated with the chords. This is the detail which needs to be mastered in order to reach the final goal. It is the final goal which is the aim of the story; namely to perform in front of a live audience. So the pupil struggling with the detail will be both motivated and connected to the final purpose, because it is being done for a reason.

Learner A was given a 12-page list of outcomes which needed to be covered in order to reach the goal. These covered things such as: knows the colour of the guitar and counts the strings of a guitar. When these were learnt, they were ticked off on the list. Learner A then moved on to the next list of things to be done. Teacher A was able to 'prove' that Learner A was progressing and was indeed moving to a higher level, because there was evidence on the tick list. When a visitor came to the school, he asked Learner A the very first question which had been set at the start of the session – 'What colour is your guitar, my friend?' But Learner A was not able to answer.

Meanwhile, Learner B was set the learning intention 'I will perform in front of a live audience.' To begin with, he strummed alongside his teacher, learning a few basic chords. Over time, his learning intentions were adjusted, adding more detail and practice, until he was able to perform in front of his friends and family. When the visitor walked in, Learner B was doing just that – 'music to my ears.'

What can we take from this, in planning for the curriculum in our own contexts? The first is that we should not make hasty judgements – for example, it is likely that Teacher B used similar practices to Teacher A. However, we need to take a hard look at what constitutes learning which ends up in the long-term memory and those activities which are proxies for learning. The critical thing is that one-off activities, which do not provide for repetition, revision and deeper understanding, are likely to be forgotten. This means that the ticks on the checklist did not actually match what the pupil could do over time. They were also time-consuming for the teacher to input. There is also a fundamental mismatch going on – it would be possible to praise Learner A for getting the correct answers, but this could have been done with very little struggle or effort. It resulted, in this instance, in learning that was transient and insecure. Learner B, by contrast, would have had to struggle, would have had to make plenty of small steps, building mastery over time. And it is this which results in learning over time.

Much of the work on mastery has been carried out in the maths curriculum. The focus has been on several elements – fluency, reasoning and problem-solving – as ways of securing deep knowledge and understanding of the principles and processes of mathematics. Mastery is not a quick fix, but a sustained and incremental process of owning and applying material over time. The simplest way to think about it is to ask; can my pupils do something, think deeply and articulate their reasoning as a result of what they have been taught?

Mastery has been described as the process of internalising and understanding a complete area of study.[1] This means congruence between the details and facts of the subject and their deeper schemata. The 'complete area of study' might be big in scope, however it might also be relatively small, but the principles remain the same. The plethora of essential facts need to be integrated in some way with the 'holding buckets' of concepts undermining the aspect of study. Mastery has implications for working memory and long-term memory. The more the basics are practised, the more secure the links with the underlying principles. There are no easy short cuts for this. It places an expectation on educators to think and plan for the underlying big ideas that need to be revisited over time. So, for fluency in maths, pupils need to know, for example, their number bonds, their times tables and have a sense of place value. They won't get these in one or two lessons. These are essential tools that are non-negotiable. As a result, they need to be revisited and revised frequently. With practice comes proficiency. And it is the proficiency which is the highway to the long-term memory. When information is secured here, it can be drawn on quickly and efficiently in new contexts.

The mastery curriculum in maths is also underpinned by reasoning and there are compelling reasons why reasoning should underpin other aspects of the curriculum, as well. Reasoning calls on us to justify, to explain and to make clear our rationale for doing something. It both draws on long-term memory and supports its nurture. When I have to explain and justify my answer to someone else, I am having to dig deeper into the underlying

---

1   psychologydictionary.org/mastery-learning-1

structures to support my argument. It is in the articulation of this process that the learning becomes embedded. The reasoning element is a way of forcing out into the open what we know intuitively, to give it voice, to make it public, so that I and others can discuss it further. Reasoning has the power to transform material into deep learning. It exposes both the strengths and flaws in an argument and makes what I have learnt visible. When it is visible, it can be critiqued, developed and praised. It provides the cement which holds organising ideas together.

The problem-solving element in the maths curriculum is a way of pupils transferring their knowledge into new areas. It compels them to recall the underlying knowledge and principles and to work out how these might apply to new work. The same also applies in other areas of the curriculum. It can be underpinned by quite simple questions such as 'where have we come across this idea before?' It is the transfer of existing knowledge into new areas which both secures the original material and opens up new vistas for further learning. The power of problems is that the answers are not immediately apparent to us. That is the point. If the answer is obvious, then it is not a problem. If we accept that we are a challenge-seeking species, that we like doing things which are difficult, then problems are a great gift to us as teachers. However, the big caveat here is that there should be high challenge, accompanied by low threat.[2]

When the conditions are right, problems open up the space for speculation, for getting things wrong, for comparing ideas. We are hard-wired to look for and enjoy things which pique our interest. This is not about making a curriculum relevant to pupils' perceived interests, rather it is about taking the subject matter as being intrinsically interesting, as the 'beating heart of the lesson'.[3] We need to accept that there will be struggles, that we and our pupils will feel frustrated at times, but that there will be pleasure from either solving a problem or having new insights into the subject material. These insights are psychologically deeply rewarding. The further power of problems is that they provide efficient mechanisms from shifting the material content from working memory through to long-term memory. The very process of engaging in the problem is helping us to traverse the twin aspects of the knowledge detail and its related concept.

---

2   www.marymyatt.com/blog/2016-01-08/high-challenge-low-threat
3   reflectingenglish.wordpress.com/author/atharby

Intellectual architecture

**'It is not the beauty of a building
you should look at; it's the
construction of the foundation
that will stand the test of time.'**
David Allan Coe

If the purpose of the new curriculum is that pupils should know things in depth then this is hard to do if they are presented with lots of information without an organising structure. If we pay attention to developing a conceptual structure, then new information from different contexts will become 'stuck' to the concept and children are able to make better sense of it. The danger with rushing through content without developing a structure is that information just floats around, unconnected. Humans seek pattern and connections and we are depriving our children of crucial intellectual development if we do not show them how information fits into a bigger whole.

Going through a lot of content gives the impression that we have covered a great deal, when in fact, all that has happened is that children have completed some exercises, a lot of them shallow, which give a superficial impression of learning. What happens when we do this is that they are not able to say, in their own words, what they have learnt and how it relates to a bigger picture. An example of this: when checking, in a faith school, the extent to which pupils knew about religions other than their own, they were able to say very little. Although they had plenty of time for religious education, they had only the odd lesson on Islam or Judaism that just dealt with a superficial knowledge of these, in very little time. When leaders were asked about the fact that the pupils appeared to know very little, they were exasperated and said that they had been taught. They showed the planning as evidence of this. The planning showed that what the children had been taught was fragmentary and 'tacked on' as an afterthought. It might have been taught, but because links had not been made with the deep concepts of religion, pupils were unable to say anything meaningful about what they had learnt about other faiths and beliefs. If, for example, they had been taught about the Muslim belief in one God, they might have been able to make the connections between Christianity and Judaism and the links in the early history between these faiths. Instead, they thought that Islam consisted of five pillars and could say nothing about them.

Children who had spent a lesson on homophones in English were asked about what they had learnt about these. Sadly, those spoken to were not able to say. They looked up at the board to read the learning objectives, stumbled over what it said and were not able to say in their own words. So it was an hour wasted because they hadn't got a clue what they were supposed to be learning. This is because moving through the curriculum content was valued more highly than checking whether pupils understood what they were doing, why it was important and how it might fit into other things they had learnt or were going to learn.

This is a waste of time and it doesn't secure children's entitlement to the curriculum. When it is seen as something to be covered rather than understood, then we have to go back to basics. And the first basic is to ask ourselves, what is the overarching idea here? What do I want my children to be able to do with this new knowledge and how will I know if they have got it? This places greater emphasis on planning and it demands responsive teaching in the lesson. Responsive teaching means fine-tuning what has been offered to pupils in light of their engagement with it. If they do not understand, it is pointless ploughing on. We need to pause and rewind. It seems to take longer at the time, but is shorter in the longer term. That is because in securing children's understanding of the basic ideas, they will move faster over time.

Let's take the concept of 'civilisation' which appears in the history curriculum for primary children. Across the primary years, they are expected to learn about a range of civilisations, and it is one of the expectations that pupils 'gain and deploy a historically grounded understanding of abstract terms such as civilisation.[1]' They will not gain an understanding of this concept if it is not taught explicitly. They will not make sense of it if the term is not used regularly as they learn about the Roman or Mayan empires, for example. All that will happen is that children will have a fragmented range of facts which do not knit together under the concept of civilisation. Their learning and potential for new learning is limited.

So it is important to spend some time unpacking what is meant by 'civilisation'[2] and for the purposes of the National Curriculum in history, this is about knowing the defining characteristics of large empires. The term 'civilisation' comes from the Latin for 'town'. The Oxford English Dictionary definition is the process by which a society or place reaches an advanced stage of social development and organisation.[3] The underlying conditions are usually in place for a civilisation to emerge: a large settlement, the existence of food surpluses to free a section of society from the need to feed itself so that they are able to produce art, administer the laws and secure order and literacy as a vehicle for myths, history, drama and philosophy. When these are in place, there is capacity for cities to grow into centres of authority, exchange and culture. In most cases, civilisation also gives rise to literate culture. By this definition, civilisation first appeared in Mesopotamia and Egypt by c.3000 BC, India by c. 2800 BC, China by about c.1500 BC; and Central and South America sometime in the first millennium BCE. From these core centres it then spread outwards, taking in most of the world by 1900 CE.[4] Pupils are entitled to have purchase on the scope and range of the concept of civilisation as they learn about specific eras in detail.

---

1   www.gov.uk/government/publications/national-curriculum-in-england-history-programmes-of-study
2   www.timemaps.com/encyclopedia/what-is-civilization
3   en.oxforddictionaries.com/definition/civilization
4   www.ancient.eu/civilization

The same applies to covenant and incarnation, for example, in religious education. And the concepts are present in each of the National Curriculum subjects. When time is taken to unpack these, to scope the landscape, to provide the bigger picture, pupils will be developing the intellectual architecture which provides the structure for the detail.

Stimulus

'Thoughts without content are empty, intuitions without concepts are blind.'
Immanuel Kant

The right stimulus helps to make concepts concrete. The right stimulus can both provide insights into new ideas and subject matter at the start of a session, or provide a focal point for applying new knowledge once a session has started. The critical thing here is that it has to be the right one and it has to be carefully chosen. If not, we are in danger of distracting from the main ideas, sending learning off in the wrong direction, or worst of all, becoming a complete distraction. A stimulus is used to stimulate thinking, not as a diversionary tactic, or for amusement or shock value.

A carefully chosen stimulus should have the potential for teachers and pupils to ask questions, to speculate, to open doors into new learning, to have multi layers which reveal further insights over time. They are not intended as a quick fix. At its simplest, in English, a text, on its own, can be, in the words of Andy Tharby, 'the beating heart of the lesson.'[1] Simple, without ornament; a piece of prose used with purpose and integrity to open up learning.

An interesting use of stimulus in history has been developed by Richard Kennett: pupils were provided with sections from a scholarly text, in this

---

1   classteaching.wordpress.com/2018/03/12/a-mastery-light-subject-curriculum-
model

example the Norman Conquest by Marc Morris.[2] Morris' text had been chosen to compare with Simon Schama's account of the same period. Pupils were expected to read extracts and to answer questions such as 'What does Morris argue most people think about the Norman Conquest?' and 'What does Morris say about the impact of the Norman Conquest on women?'[3] The careful use of a stimulus for these pupils took them into demanding work. It was neither gimmicky, nor complicated. The task was characterized by high challenge and low threat: 'Read these and answer all the questions. This is supposed to be hard. If you can't answer all the questions don't worry!'

An underestimated resource is that of photographs as stimuli. When beamed through onto a screen, they can provide a starting point which is both high challenge and low threat. This means that there is challenge, first in interpreting the image, for its superficial impression, then looking for deeper meaning. It is low threat, because any response which is honest and relevant is appropriate. A photograph, or indeed a piece of artwork, can open up deep responses, which are first articulated, discussed and then, if appropriate, written down. A very good example in one primary school was the use of 'The Guardian Eyewitness'[4] series, where images of exceptional quality through a lens on world events are shown through the prism of high-quality photography. In this school, the lead for religious education was concerned that parents were reluctant for their children to visit the local gurdwaras and were clear that they did not want their children learning about Islam.

There were concerns that if the school tried to insist that the children had these experiences (when parents are, in fact, entitled to withdraw their pupils from religious education) it could entrench positions. So instead, what this teacher did was to select images from 'The Guardian Eyewitness', some of which showed religious events and festivals, and some which showed people from different cultures. These were shown through the whiteboard, without captions. Rather than making the case, important though it is, that all children should encounter a rounded experience of the subject, they simply showed these images and asked the children to look at them while they drank after their break. There was no expectation that they had to respond. However, after a week or so

2   Morris, M. (2013) *The Norman Conquest*, Windmill Books.
3   twitter.com/kenradical/status/997402953475674112
4   www.theguardian.com/world/series/eyewitness

of being shown these photographs, children started to make comments, such as 'I wonder what they are doing?' or 'I wonder where they come from?' *etc. etc.* So then they were offered sticky notes on tables, and could write their questions or comments on these, if they chose to do so. These questions, over time, became the focus for further work in lessons, some of which related to RE, and some to geography, art *etc.* So successful was the careful use of these photographs, without prejudging or any expectations on the part of the pupils, that the 10 minute sessions were established as part of the regular timetable and routine and were renamed 'drink and think' sessions.

Artefacts, or pieces of material related to the subject under exploration, also have great potential for securing knowledge in the long-term memory. Holding a menorah or mezuzah in a religious education lesson, or handling gas masks from a local museum in history or pottery from the Mediterranean in a geography lesson, for example, are all shorthand, powerful ways of opening up discussions. Where it is not possible to handle artefacts, photographs of these can provide a second-hand experience. For example, the exceptional resources at the British Museum, in particular 'A history of the world in 100 objects',[5] the British Library, where it is possible to look at religious and other texts in detail[6] and the National Gallery's 'Take One Picture'[7] all provide powerful stimuli for discussion and learning.

Careful selection of stimuli can also expand earlier learning. For instance, Doug Lemov proposes additional stimuli such as articles on caste systems, gender roles, the American Dream and the Dust Bowl and migration from the Great Plains, which expand on the themes in Esperanza Rising.[8] These build background knowledge and help bring the text to life in richness and depth. Through this simple exercise, pupils are offered material which provides cognitive challenge and helps them make connections, thereby securing the knowledge and wider concepts in the long-term memory.

---

5   www.britishmuseum.org/explore/a_history_of_the_world.aspx
6   www.bl.uk/onlinegallery/sacredtexts
7   www.nationalgallery.org.uk/learning/teachers-and-schools/take-one-picture
8   en.wikipedia.org/wiki/Esperanza_Rising

Knowledge organisers

'An investment in knowledge pays the best interest.'
Benjamin Franklin

Knowledge organisers are designed to do exactly what it says on the tin. Developed by Joe Kirby[1] and colleagues at the Michaela School, they capture the key information, date lines, quotes and terminology for a topic. They are usually one side of A4, which is important as the material to be learnt and mastered needs to be tight. The understanding is that this is the minimum that needs to be known, rehearsed and stored over time in the long-term memory, in order for pupils to become fluent in the material. It is a given that plenty of other technical vocabulary and facts will be encountered and learnt through the topic. The material on the organiser is necessary, but not sufficient for gaining deep knowledge over time.

The real power of knowledge organisers is that they make us think hard about what we are going to teach. This might sound like a statement of the obvious; of course we all think about what we are going to be teaching.

---

1   pragmaticreform.wordpress.com/2015/03/28/knowledge-organisers

89

However, the work on preparing a knowledge organiser requires a level of discipline to ask ourselves the following: what are the overarching themes or timeline for this unit? What is the key technical vocabulary? What are the key quotes that will exemplify the subject? It is the paring down to the essentials that brings rigour and discipline. It also makes planning and the setting of homework much more straightforward.[2]

They also have the benefit of honesty and simplicity. They lay down the territory up front and let pupils know that these are the non-negotiables in order for them to succeed. They are not expected to know the content from the word go, but rather incrementally over time. This supports resilience, as the expectation is that all pupils will gain ownership of these over time. This is done by setting some to be learnt for homework, revisiting in class and low stakes testing. The message, that this is to be mastered over time, is a very powerful one for pupils – it conveys the idea that we all start somewhere, that we all get better with practice and it is fine to get things wrong. In fact, it is quite important to make mistakes, as it is in the revising and checking for the correct answer that learning is deepened. Indeed, if the key facts are known too soon, if there isn't sufficient struggle, then the learning will be less secure.

A note on the use of the content in knowledge organisers: many schools ask pupils to learn a number of facts or key words for homework. The number will depend on the complexity of the material and the age of the pupils. These are then tested in the next lesson. The important thing here is that the tests are high challenge, in the sense that they are expecting pupils to recall the information, but they are low threat, in that the results are private to the pupil and teacher. The 'testing effect'[3] is the finding that there are gains in long-term memory and retention of knowledge by active retrieval through testing. Such testing has nothing to do with grades or extensive feedback. If the tests are done on a regular basis, pupils will be able to see the progress they have made, over time. This is deeply satisfying, helps build confidence and means that pupils are more likely to persevere with difficult material, when they understand that it can be mastered, over time.

---

2   primaryknowledgeorganisers.wordpress.com/geuifger
3   Abel, M. & Roediger, H. L. (2017)Comparing the testing effect under blocked and mixed practice: The mnemonic benefits of retrieval practice are not affected by practice format, *Memory & Cognition*, 45 (1), pp81-92.

The downside to organisers is when they are used as ends in themselves. They should be viewed as the starting points for the topic being learnt. It is not helpful if they are seen as the latest, short-cut fix for planning. While it is fine to use those that have been prepared by other schools or professionals, these should be adapted for individual units of work. The best practice, as in Clare Sealy's school in London,[4] is where the principles of knowledge organisers are shared and debated with staff. They created their own, adapted those already available, and, crucially, revisited them in the light of experience. They became an element in professional development, rather than an add-on. Used in this way, they are important tools for continuing professional development.

So, if considering using knowledge organisers, where is a good place to start? It is worth looking to see what is already available, to note how they are structured. Generally, they include the following: key dates, quotes, technical vocabulary, concepts, key figures and timelines where appropriate.

If the ones considered are similar to the topic being planned, they can be used and adapted if necessary. However, given that none of us will be experts ourselves in the subject matter and material for every unit we need to teach, it is important that our own subject knowledge is brought up to speed. This is particularly important if we are adapting existing knowledge organisers, rather than coming up with our own. This does not mean that we have to research to the level of a PhD, but it does mean that we have to do some headline reading and think carefully about the wider context of the key concepts and knowledge within the organisers. This is best done with others. It not only makes it more efficient, it also supports professional learning. At Shaun Allison's school, Durrington, teachers meet every fortnight to discuss the content of what is to be taught and how best to deliver it.[5] In smaller schools, this might not be possible. However, schools should be able to arrange virtual sharing of planning with colleagues who are doing similar work in other schools. This takes some thought, but particularly with schools working in partnership either as MATs or federations or teaching schools, the potential for making and using networks is there, we just have to make use of it.

---

4   primarytimery.com/2017/07/30/the-highs-and-lows-of-knowledge-organisers-
      an-end-of-year-report
5   classteaching.wordpress.com/2016/09/19/subject-planning-and-development-
      sessions

To summarise the importance of key knowledge: 'One of the most important principles of psychology is that knowledge builds on knowledge. The more you know, the more readily you can learn something new, because you have a lot more analogies and points of contact for connecting the new knowledge with what you already know. The more you know, the smarter you are. Our students become more intelligent when they know more. So does everybody. Researchers have been telling us this fact about human intelligence for many years. Intelligence increases with knowledge. General knowledge is the best single tool in a person's intellectual armory.'[6]

---

6   Hirsch, E. D. (1999) *The Schools We Need: And Why We Don't Have Them*, Anchor Books.

Vocabulary

'Vocabulary is a matter of word-building as well as word-using.'
David Crystal

Deliberately building vocabulary is one of the most important things we can do as teachers. It is important for several reasons. The first is that if we are serious about closing the gap between those pupils who come from language-rich backgrounds and those who do not, then we need to pay careful attention to the building of vocabulary. The second is that is a deepening and extension of knowledge. And finally, there is the sheer joy of words well-used. As Isabel Beck argues[1] 'a rich vocabulary supports learning about the world, encountering new ideas, enjoying the beauty of language. A rich vocabulary enhances an interview, allows one to see the humour in word play, shores up what an individual wants to say, and, especially, wants to write.'

There is plenty of evidence that a wide vocabulary is closely related to good reading comprehension. The flip side to this is that a lack of vocabulary can 'hold back pupils' ability to think, speak, read, comprehend and write about a topic or concept...one of the main reasons pupils are below their grade level in their reading proficiency and struggle to catch up is their

---

1   Beck *et al*, (2013) *Bringing Words to Life: Robust Vocabulary Instruction*. Guilford Press.

vocabulary deficits.'[2] In Laura Robb's survey[3] of American teachers, she found that all agreed that vocabulary building was important for all pupils, and particularly so for those from word-poor backgrounds. However, she also found that explicit teaching of vocabulary was sporadic rather than systematic. I believe there is a similar picture in this country. Vocabulary building is agreed to be beneficial, but when asking the extent to which there is explicit teaching of vocabulary before, during and/or after reading, there is less certainty. There is an assumption that exposure is sufficient. Well it might be for some pupils some of the time, but we need to get to a stage where new words are taught explicitly to all children. Otherwise, there is a danger that some will miss out.

There is evidence that pre-teaching some vocabulary has considerable benefits, because reading about an unfamiliar topic with no prior knowledge is exhausting and discouraging.[4] If pupils are to move beyond the surface meaning of words, they need to meet them in reading, listening and discussion. And pre-teaching starts this process. Pre-teaching includes the context and examples of the words and definitions, rather than just the words themselves. If we just focus on teaching the individual words and pupils learning these without context, we are likely to be placing too great a burden on their working memory. We need to identify the words, capture the essence of them and explain them in everyday language, followed by an example. This takes time, but if we are serious about developing vocabulary beyond the everyday, it is important.

So what are the words that are worth pre-teaching, highlighting, talking about and ensuring that our pupils learn? Well, it is helpful to use the 'Three Tier' model developed by Isobel Beck, Margaret McKeown and Linda Kucan[5] as a means to identify vocabulary which pupils need to know. Tier one consists of approximately 5500 high-frequency words which need little direct instruction because they are common in daily use. Tier two is general academic words which occur across different subjects and which are essential to reading comprehension – words such as analyse, complex,

---

2   Robb, L. (2014) *Vocabulary Is Comprehension: Getting to the Root of Text Complexity*, Corwin Press.
3   *op. cit.*
4   www.literacyworldwide.org/blog/literacy-daily/2013/06/06/cold-versus-warm-close-reading-stamina-and-the-accumulation-of-misdirection
5   *op. cit.*

clarify, hypothesis. Tier three is subject-specific words such as isotope, economics, algebra, decimal, idiom, sonnet, civilisation.

Beck *et al* recommend finding Tier two words in class readers, and then, when you've read the chapter in which the words occur, doing some specific work on those words. They recommend that instead of using dictionary definitions, you use longer definitions that could be more accurately described as explanations, and that you present pupils with the word being used in different contexts.

As Katie Ashford argues, 'the words that will have the biggest impact on a child's vocabulary are words that you see often in books, but hear rarely in speech. Words such as: derive, evoke, surreptitious, capricious, incredulous and eradicate all fall into this category. Focus on these sorts of words and pupils' vocabularies will increase over time. This works because in order to learn new words, you need to know other words. The more of these words you are taught, the easier it is to learn other words. It's a lovely, virtuous cycle.'[6] Alex Quigley's work on closing the vocabulary gap makes the case that the increased demands of an academic curriculum means it is imperative to close the gap between the 'word poor' and the 'word rich' and that this is a priority for teachers of all subjects across the curriculum.[7]

There is a problem with just expecting pupils to use a dictionary, because often the definitions are too abstract, vague or can be confusing. Let's take the example of 'illusion'.[8] The dictionary definition, 'appearance or feeling that misleads because it is not real', is too vague. An 'appearance that misleads' is rather hard to make sense of. Might it be something that looks good but isn't – like a stale piece of cake? Or considering 'feeling' – how does a feeling mislead? How is a feeling not real? The core of illusion is something that looks real but isn't, or appears to be something but isn't there at all. Those ideas could be put together in a definition such as 'something that looks like one thing but is really something else or is not there at all.' And it is in the discussion of these subtleties that insights and deep understanding reside.

---

6   tabularasaeducation.wordpress.com/2015/04/03/vocab
7   Quigley,A (2018) *Closing the Vocabulary Gap*, Routledge.
8   *op. cit.*

Etymology

'Names, once they are in common use, quickly become mere sounds, their etymology being buried, like so many of the earth's marvels, beneath the dust of habit.'
Salman Rushdie

If the purpose of curriculum design is to ensure that pupils have access to and master deep subject knowledge, then one of the most efficient ways of doing this is to expose them to the technical vocabulary and subject-specific terminology of a subject area. Doing this creates a key which unlocks the territory of the domain. The subject-specific vocabulary often has ancient roots, usually Latin and Greek. There is a temptation to think that these are too difficult for pupils to learn and to use confidently. This should not be the case. All pupils are entitled to be exposed to the richness of vocabulary, including where those words come from. If we are not prepared to do this, we are denying them the chance to fully enter the academic discipline.

There are children as young as four who are 'fluent' in dinosaurs. Many take great pleasure in pronouncing the names of different dinosaurs. Some even know that the word 'dinosaur' comes from the ancient Greek, meaning 'scary' or 'terrible' (deinos) lizard (sauros). What happens when they are making connections between the root or roots of a word, is that they are creating a larger picture of meaning. In doing this, they are making links to the long-term memory, because it is another layer of a story which connects back to the word. If very young children are able to do this, and take great pleasure from it, then we should not shy away from unpicking, delving and finding out the etymological roots of words. Every subject has them, and we do not need to be classicists to support our children in this.

A further reason why etymological work is important is that the key words within a subject area are often conceptual. This means that they are often the 'holding baskets' for a lot of small details of knowledge. If pupils have access to, understand and are able to use the conceptual, technical vocabulary expertly and confidently, we are leading them into the territory of long-term memory. In addition, when we are planning learning, it is important and efficient to identify the key concepts we want pupils to learn. So identifying these and doing work around their original meanings will take pupils deeper into the richness of the subject.

So, for instance, when thinking about planning a unit of work about Christianity in Key Stage 1, one group of teachers working together decided that one of the key concepts it was important for pupils to know and learn was 'incarnation'. They identified this, because it is a fundamental belief within the Christian community that the divine became human in the form of Jesus. They realised that without this knowledge, pupils' learning could be fragmented. As a result, they explored the etymology of 'incarnation' – they talked about how it comes from the Latin, a language spoken across the Roman empire. They talked about the legacy of Latin which means that many words in English and other languages have traces of Latin in them. So 'in' for example, means 'in' both in Latin and English. The 'carnation' part of the word comes from the Latin 'carnis', which means flesh. It is the same root in the words carnation, chilli con carne and carnival, as well as many others.

Using this knowledge, teachers were able to explain to their pupils that Christians believe that God became human and that is why the word 'incarnation' is so important. Then, when they went on to learn about advent and Christmas, pupils were able to place that knowledge within the conceptual basket of incarnation and were able to say that Christmas is important to Christians because it is the time when God gave the gift of a son in the form of baby Jesus. And that is why it is celebrated and we have the tradition of giving one another presents, whether we are religious or not. Now, the important thing here, is not that pupils have to be religious themselves to make sense of this, nor is there any purpose of proselytizing, rather, that pupils have a grasp of the underlying concept into which they can put their knowledge; in this case, about the birth of Jesus. And a similar exercise was done for Easter, where the underlying concept was identified as 'salvation'. Once pupils know and understand the root of salvation, meaning 'to save', they are able to make the connections with Jesus' death and resurrection. This, in turn, links to the symbolism of Easter eggs and the religious symbolism for new life.

The potential for etymological exploration exists in every subject area. When we expose pupils to these and expect them to engage with the roots of words, we are supporting them to enter into the world of academic discourse. This is not to say that they will immediately be experts, but what they will have are the tools, which will be developed over time, to support them in developing expertise. Furthermore, many root words are found in different contexts. For example, the word 'isosceles' comes from the ancient Greek for 'equal' (isos) and 'legs' (sceles). If pupils have done work on the etymology of isosceles, not only will they have a picture in their minds which is more concrete than the abstract term, they will also have the ability to recognise 'isos' when them come across it elsewhere – for example in isobar, isometric. It is giving them the tools both for deeper learning in the immediate context, tools which can be transferred elsewhere, and which provide great pleasure in the process.

Many of the key words identified in a knowledge organiser will have roots from other languages. Words such as 'algebra' (Arabic), 'sabotage' (French) as well as much of the technical vocabulary in all subject areas which have their origins in Latin and Greek are opportunities for homework and light-touch research. It is important that teachers do not feel they have to be classicists or linguists themselves. All that is needed is to say, 'This is an interesting word. I wonder where it comes from? Could you find out?' With a bit of guidance on how to find the etymology by typing the word into a search engine followed by 'etymology' (which means 'true word' in Greek), pupils can do this for themselves.

The final argument for addressing etymology is that it is an efficient way of extending pupils' vocabulary. The study of roots and affixes extends vocabulary because they have the potential to learn further words as a result of these. Since 90% of English words of two or more syllables have Latin and Greek roots, it is vital that this type of word study is incorporated into all subjects.[1]

---

1   Nichols, W. D, Rupley, W. H. & Rasinski, T. (2008) Fluency in Learning to Read for Meaning: Going Beyond Repeated Readings, *Literacy Research and Instruction*, 48 (1), 1-13, DOI: 10.1080/19388070802161906

Visits and visitors

'The bits I most remember about my school days are those that took place outside the classroom, as we were taken on countless theatre visits and trips to places of interest.'
Alan Bennett

The purpose of visits and visitors is to cement the curriculum, not as a jolly add-on. Both visits and visitors can enhance and deepen knowledge, but only if they are planned and contiguous to the subject. However, too many visits and visitors are stand-alone activities. When this happens, it means missed opportunities for learning. Visits and visitors provide opportunities for generating questions, further research and extended writing opportunities. They can often be the trigger for bringing aspects of the curriculum to life and to support long-standing learning. So, what are some of the opportunities and how might they be used?

To start with; potential visitors from the local community. Wherever a school is located, it will have a richness of local voices and views from which robust learning can take place. In geography, for example, at Key Stage 2, pupils are expected to study aspects of their local area. This is an opportunity to make contact with older members of a community, who can talk to pupils about how the locality has changed in their lifetime. The Women's Institute or parish council are likely to have contacts who would provide lively accounts of the change in the locality over time.

Parents and extended family members, as part of the school community, are often an untapped resource for exploring aspects of the curriculum. This could be in terms of hearing about the range of jobs and occupations, hobbies or areas of expertise. Victoria Park Academy in Birmingham has been particularly skilful in drawing on the rich resources of parents and extended families. Many come from Bangladesh and their stories and culinary wisdom has been used to inform the extended curriculum. Ballot Street Spice is the result – a combination of imaginative curriculum planning which embeds food technology, geography and enterprise and an authentic use of the local community as a resource. The result is an award-winning social enterprise which deepens elements of the curriculum and generates income for the school. Its strapline is, 'Blending spices to create opportunity.'[1]

Sometimes a specialist might be needed and they might not be available locally. In which case, it is possible to arrange either Skype calls or emails with experts. If time constraints are difficult, pupils could create their questions and ask the expert to produce a video in response. Most people are happy to be asked to contribute. It is, after all, a compliment to be thought of as an expert in something.

There are also online resources such as 'Email a Believer'[2] from REonline.[3] This is particularly helpful for those schools which draw on monocultural communities, away from cities and large populations. Here, pupils can check which questions have already been asked and answered. And if they have something which has not been addressed, they can send over their question. The believer then responds. The service also has humanist and pagan responders as well.

And what about links with other pupils in other parts of the country and around the world? Why shouldn't the visitors, whether in person or through the internet, be children of similar age, through projects like PenPals Schools?[4]

---

1   ballotstreet.co.uk
2   pof.reonline.org.uk
3   www.reonline.org.uk
4   www.penpalschools.com

Every school, whatever its locality, will have places of worship. Many religious communities see education as part of their role – not to proselytize but to educate and inform. Many are happy to host visits to churches, synagogues, mosques, gurdwaras and shrines, amongst others, and are prepared to talk to pupils as 'experts' in the lived experience of their faith.

The notion of visits does not need to be an expensive, complicated piece of work. In every locality, there will be ponds, open space and, if lucky, rivers or the seaside. And yet, how often are these overlooked as sources, both for cementing the curriculum and for utter delight? Visits to any of these could support work in geography, science, history, art, English... what is stopping us from seeing their potential and using them? And the beautiful thing about opening up to the possibilities of our local landscape and cityscape is that much of it can be done on foot. No expense, only some time. In fact, I would argue that visits should be part of every child's entitlement – every year group should have at least one visit to a local place of interest, however simple and humble, as part of their experience.

Further afield, in many local towns and cities, there are museums, art galleries and civic spaces which can be used to bring the curriculum to life. Not in an artificial way, but in a way that brings scholarship to life. And the great metropolitan cities of the regions, including the capital, all have the potential to be capitalised on. Funding is likely to be an issue here, but what would it take for a commitment to be made for every child to visit somewhere significant, out of the normal experience, at least once in a key stage? Might some pupil premium funding be used for this? And if money is still a barrier, then virtual access to these great centres and repositories can be made via the internet. And the Council for Learning Outside the Classroom[5] has advice on the range of places which support learning, back in the classroom.

And it is worth just considering how the environment right around the school can be used for learning: there is usually a place of worship within walking distance, schools by the coast have the shoreline and there are natural habitats near most schools, even in cities. It's important to let children explore, breathe fresh air and take that learning back to the classroom. West Rise Junior in East Sussex knows exactly how to do this

---

5   www.lotc.org.uk

– it uses the locality to extend and enrich learning and is not afraid to play with fire as part of this![6]

Planning visits and visitors are also curriculum opportunities. Pupils can research local places of interest and potential visitors. They can work out what the costs, if any, might be; they can research the health and safety considerations, draft letters of invitation, draft letters of consent to parents and guardians. And all this is authentic writing for a purpose.

---

6   www.theguardian.com/education/2016/oct/04/school-guns-knives-fire-ofsted-danger

Section 5:
Across the
Curriculum

Speaking

'Every teacher is a teacher of English because every teacher is a teacher in English. We cannot give a lesson in any subject without helping or neglecting the English of our pupils.'
George Sampson

Literacy is an ugly word with unhelpful connotations, as Geoff Barton pointed out.[1]But never mind. In a school context, it constitutes speaking, listening, reading and writing. Literacy across the curriculum has more traction than numeracy. This is because literacy underpins every aspect of the teaching and learning, in a way that numeracy doesn't. Most schools have a literacy policy and most teachers and subject areas reflect this in their planning. However, I'm going to make the case that we do not, as a sector, spend nearly enough time on the first. That's right: speaking. Why is this? I suspect it is because speaking is something virtually all of us do, as it is the common currency of human transactions and interactions. And so, it is taken for granted. But we need to pay more attention to it, because it is the development of talk which underpins everything else: all learning, including reading and writing.

---

1   Barton, G. (2012) *Don't Call It Literacy*, Routledge.

I don't think that much has changed since the 1975 Bullock Report identified a close attention to speech being fundamental to cognitive development within a subject: 'In general, a curriculum subject, philosophically speaking, is a distinctive mode of analysis. While many teachers recognise that their aim is to initiate a student in a particular mode of analysis, they rarely recognise the linguistic implications of doing so. They do not recognise, in short, that the mental processes they seek to foster are the outcome of a development that originates in speech.'[2] Now, in many classrooms, teachers put up the key technical vocabulary, but often neglect to refer to it or expect their pupils to use it. It is as though pupils will somehow absorb it without it being taught explicitly and without the expectation that pupils will practise using it. And this is usually because of the mistaken belief that they have to get to the written work quickly.

The paradox is that written work will be of higher quality if there has been high-quality talk, using subject-specific vocabulary prior to the writing. As Neil Mercer argues,[3] talk needs tuition. There are, as ever, examples of high-quality practice, for example at the Durrington school, where there is a purposeful focus on finding 'bright spots' in classrooms. This attention to the aspects which are working well and which have the greatest impact on learning builds capacity and encourages others to think how they might do the same. And what is really helpful is that the deputy head, Shaun Allison, writes up brief blog posts to share what has been found: for example in this post[4] he and his colleague have identified, among other things, that teachers are ensuring that pupils are using the correct technical vocabulary, for example 'erosion' rather than 'worn away' in geography, and explicit use of technical vocabulary in a science lesson. This way of working slows things down in the short term, however, it has greater impact, in that through the talk, pupils have a deeper understanding of the academic domains.

So, if talk is fundamental to formulating ideas, speculating, working out mistakes and misconceptions, then we need to provide opportunities for this to be built into curriculum planning. The problem with speaking

---

2   DES. (1975) A Language for Life: report of the committee of inquiry appointed by the Secretary of State for Education and Science and the chairmanship of Sir Alan Bullock FBA, London, HMSO, para 12.4. www.educationengland.org.uk/documents/bullock/bullock1975.html
3   www.cam.ac.uk/research/discussion/why-teach-oracy
4   classteaching.wordpress.com/2016/01/24/bright-spots-22-january-2016

and listening is that they do not lend themselves to being captured on a spreadsheet. We need to forget about the spreadsheet and just crack on with it. There is an assumption that pupils will just 'get it'. But they won't get it and they certainly won't get better at speaking, unless we teach them. If we know that many pupils from disadvantaged backgrounds have not had as many stories, songs and poems read to them, then their language acquisition needs strengthening. We have to be careful not to stereotype here, because many pupils from disadvantaged backgrounds do have these simple, deep experiences. Yet, as a cohort, there is plenty of evidence that the exposure to rich language needs building up. There is nothing we can do about what happens in the home, or in wider society, but there is plenty we can do once they are in our schools and classrooms.

From a very early age, pupils should be encouraged to use full sentences, using technical vocabulary. Too often, we are inclined to complete sentences for them, so that we can move on to the next thing. When this happens, we are taking away part of their learning. They have a right and an entitlement to talk about what they know, understand and do. We hold our children to account on what they write; we should be doing the same for how they speak. When we get this right, they are going to produce richer, more proficient writing in any case. But the talk has to precede the writing.

We also need to expose children to technical vocabulary at a young age. Why? Because they are entitled to it and because they can cope with it. When they have the chance to make connections and play with words and their meaning, they are building a richness of academic language will support their long-term memory, engrain a fascination with words and in the process become fluent and confident speakers.

James Britton has pointed out that we use language to categorise. This is because it is an efficient way of making sense of describing the world and communicating with others. There are, for example, apparently seven million distinguishable colours, but we mostly, not always, simplify these into red, green *etc.* If we didn't, we'd spend all day describing the particular redness of red. And so we rely on the process of classification; 'experience is kaleidoscopic: the experience of every moment is unique and unrepeatable. Until we can group items in it on the basis of their similarity we can set up no expectations, make no predictions.'[5]

---

5   Britton, J. (1970) *Language and Learning*, Penguin.

He goes on to argue that 'it is the existence of classes at different levels of generality that finally makes possible the highest forms of thought process, including what we call reasoning.[6]' Now this is important, very important. If a child comes to school, not having had the opportunity to experience basic generalisations, for example, that a buttercup represents a class of objects that is a subclass of that represented by 'flower', and that this, in turn, is a subclass of the class of objects represented by 'plants', then they are going to miss out. And if we don't want them to miss out, we need to privilege language and talk throughout every phase of the sector. Language is the cornerstone of reasoning.

A few words on listening. There are two aspects to this – one is to listen and the other is to be listened to. It is one of our deepest needs to be heard. When we pay attention to what someone says, we are paying them a big compliment. We are honouring them and their ideas. Children need to learn the importance of this. At an intellectual level, when I listen to someone I am learning from them.

So listening is more than good manners, it is a building block through which my own knowledge and understanding grows. In a classroom where 'no hands up' is a regular feature, it means that anyone in the group or class, can be called on. By ensuring 'no hands up' it keeps everyone on their toes as any pupil can be asked, at any time, for their response. And there is also an expectation that pupils will listen carefully to what others are saying so that they are able to build on the answers or provide an alternative point of view. The caveat to this is that we do not call on the child who cannot cope at that point – this could be because of a recent upset or worse. So we need to be sensitive to who we call on, and if we know that we are not going to be asking a pupil at that point, we will still make sure that they are paying attention and listening to what others are contributing.

There is a further element to listening and it relates to the teacher. If pupils are expected to develop their capacity to talk well, then the adults need to listen carefully to what pupils say. And, of course, the response to this might be, that we already do listen to what pupils say in classrooms. However, I don't think that we spend enough time thinking about the quality of professional listening. This is important, because I cannot expand on, probe and challenge pupils' responses unless I am paying

---

6   *op. cit.*

careful attention to what is being said. And when this close attention and response to pupils is in place, then I am more likely to shift towards cognitively challenging dialogue.[7]

There are some barriers to prioritising speaking and listening: there is a reluctance to expect shy and under-confident pupils to make an oral contribution in case they struggle. Sometimes it is a case of prioritising other tasks and, in particular, pupils' writing. Sometimes teachers lack confidence and expertise in developing speaking and listening and this has not been helped by the lack of training. As Robin Alexander says[8] 'One of the reasons why talk is undervalued in British education is that there is a tendency to see its function as primarily social, as mainly about the acquisition of confidence in the business of communicating with others... but as psychologists, neuroscientists, anthropologists and classroom researchers have long understood, the function of talk in classrooms is cognitive and cultural as well as social.'

Organisations such as Voice21 have developed high-quality resources and training[9] which builds on the work of School21. It is worth watching the videos of the high-quality talk and listening from pupils at the school.[10] This work builds on Robin Alexander's 'Dialogic Teaching', which makes the case for the power of talk to stimulate and extend students' thinking and advance their learning and understanding.[11] So let's shift away from the perception that oracy is a by-product of classroom activity, or relevant only in certain subjects such as English: 'We want children to find their voice metaphorically & literally.'[12]

And yet, while we know that the sector is not consistent in promoting high-quality talk, there are, nevertheless, examples of schools who are bucking the trend. In the 2016 report by Will Millard and Loic Menzies, *Oracy: The State of Speaking in Our Schools*, LKMco[13] there is a careful analysis both of some of the barriers and some of the opportunities for developing talk in schools.

And finally, from Richard Sennett: 'Dialectic and dialogic procedures

---

7   www.tandfonline.com/doi/abs/10.1207/S15326950DP3502_3
8   www.robinalexander.org.uk/dialogic-teaching
9   www.voice21.org
10 www.school21.org.uk/voice21
11 www.robinalexander.org.uk/dialogic-teaching
12 Peter Hyman, Executive Head, School 21: www.voice21.org
13 www.lkmco.org/oracy-state-speaking-schools

offer two ways of practising a conversation, the one by play of contraries leading to agreement, the other by bouncing off views and experiences in an open-ended way.'[14] So, if we want to create the conditions for confident learners who are able to think and write clearly, we need to pay far more attention to talk and the quality of talk.

---

14   Sennett, R. (2012) *Together: The Rituals, Pleasures and Politics of Cooperation*, Allen Lane.

Reading across the curriculum

'There's so much more to a book than just the reading.'
Maurice Sendak

Yes indeed – there is a whole lot more to a book than just reading. Reading is a gateway into unfamiliar places, other people and alternative experiences. There are three aspects to reading in schools: the first is the teaching of reading, the second is reading in subjects beyond English and the third is reading for pleasure.

By way of background, it is important to refer to some of the research in cognitive science which helps us make the case for reading. Annie Murphy Paul[1] has made the case that 'the brain, it seems, does not make much of a distinction between reading about an experience and encountering it in real life; in each case, the same neurological regions are stimulated.' Fiction, Keith Oatley[2] notes, 'is a particularly useful simulation, because negotiating the social world effectively is extremely tricky, requiring us to weigh up myriad interacting instances of cause and effect. Just as

---

1   www.nytimes.com/2012/03/18/opinion/sunday/the-neuroscience-of-your-brain-on-fiction.html
2   en.wikipedia.org/wiki/Keith_Oatley

computer simulations can help us get to grips with complex problems such as flying a plane or forecasting the weather, so novels, stories and dramas can help us understand the complexities of social life.'

In 'Reading Reconsidered'[3] Doug Lemon makes the case that 'we are strong believers in the "power of the book", of students building a sustained relationship with a text over time and coming to understand its perspective and modes of narration, and how they shift. In fact, only by glimpsing these changes and variations as part of a sustained relationship between reader and text can students really learn to read.' He argues that the most successful schools and teachers consistently opt for books of substance as the core of their instructional choices. Furthermore, Daniel Willingham argues that one of the strongest drivers of reading ability is prior knowledge: once pupils are fluent decoders, much of the difference among readers is not due to whether you are a good or bad reader. Much of the difference among readers is due to how much knowledge they have. 'Teaching content is teaching reading.'[4]

The pity with reading in many schools is that it is often limited to timetabled variations on guided reading. Many secondary schools are now including silent reading in tutor time, but when asked about the quality of the books read and the extent to which pupils are expected to share their opinions on what they are reading, there is less clarity. And yet there are many opportunities for reading high-quality texts in lessons. In fact, if we are serious about building knowledge and vocabulary, then opportunities and expectations for reading need to be higher. The Michaela School recognises this – they estimate that their pupils read in the region of 8000 words a day[5] because they recognise that reading builds knowledge, and, as a by-product, pupils' enjoyment. There is a powerful anecdote on the blog about pupils asking to be read 'Adrian Mole' because they heard that another class was having it read to them by their teacher.

There are two further aspects to reading and the first is reading for pleasure. The OECD report 'Reading for Change'[6] found a high correlation between reading enjoyment and educational success. In fact, this mattered more than a child's social and economic background. The difference in

---

3   Lemov,D. *et al* (2016) *A Practical Guide to Rigorous Literacy Instruction*, Jossey-Bass.
4   Willingham,D. (2010) *Why Don't Students Like School?* Jossey-Bass.
5   mcsbrent.co.uk/english-how-should-we-read-texts-in-lessons
6   www.oecd.org/education/school/
    programmeforinternationalstudentassessmentpisa/33690986.pdf

reading ability between a child who reads for pleasure for 30 minutes a day and one who never reads was more than a year. Similarly, the DfE's 'Research evidence on reading for pleasure'[7] came to similar conclusions. Clare Sealy[8] has written about how provision is made for high-quality reading in her school. This involves careful consideration of where children have access to books – for example, they have moved many of the library books into classrooms so that teachers can support children in selecting their books.

If we are serious about literacy across the curriculum, we need to be considering what other texts pupils should be exposed to beyond literature, important as these are. Do they have the chance to read widely in history, geography, art, religious education? Or do we limit their diet to gobbets downloaded from the internet? A helpful site, Books for Topics[9] suggests reading books and texts to support topics in history, geography, science and other areas of the curriculum across primary. If we want to improve reading, these books should not be 'nice to have' but fundamental to growing the knowledge, vocabulary and ideas related to that subject.

Teresa Cremin's research[10] on reading for pleasure pedagogy at the Open University has identified the elements in helping children to read for pleasure, where teachers take responsibility for and plan to develop children's reading for pleasure alongside and as complementary to reading instruction; they effectively use their wider knowledge of children's literature and other texts to enrich children's experience and pleasure in reading; let children control more of their own reading and exercise their rights as readers; make time and space for children to explore texts in greater depth; share favourites and talk spontaneously about their reading. Both Clare Sealy and Jonny Walker[11] make the case that a broad knowledge on the part of the teacher is essential. Then they can make recommendations and stretch the territory of what a child might otherwise stick to.

---

7   www.gov.uk/government/uploads/system/uploads/attachment_data/
file/284286/reading_for_pleasure.pdf
8   primarytimery.com/2018/02/25/reading-for-pleasure-a-different-king-of-rigour
9   www.booksfortopics.com
10 www.researchrichpedagogies.org/research/theme/reading-for-pleasure-
pedagogy
11 jonnywalkerteaching.wordpress.com/2018/02/24/shelf-life

Teresa Cremin argues that teachers should talk about all the material they are reading and that this should more than bound books. If we think this is important, then teachers need to be given time to read. Clare Sealy estimates that a teacher in upper Key Stage 2 should be reading about one children's novel a fortnight in order to keep up with their subject knowledge. She has provided inset time to give them a head start on this.

There is one neglected aspect to reading for pleasure and this is being read to for pleasure. Clare Sealy describes how important this is, particularly for the 20% of children who are not read to at home. It is worth quoting in full: 'We need to help children build an emotional relationship with books: the Readit2[12] project helps to do this in early years. And that means trying to replicate, as far as one can in a classroom with 30 children, the experience of snuggling up with a trusted adult and a wonderful book. The snuggling is probably going to be metaphorical, but story time needs to try and emulate at least some of the intimacy and bonding that goes on when a child shares a book with their parent at bed time. Talking about the book together is important – how else will children realise that reading can be an enjoyable social activity? But make sure this does not turn into another literacy lesson.'[13]Yes, well quite.

So let's take the advice of Michael Morpurgo: 'Let there be half an hour of story time at the end of school in primary schools. Make this the half hour they all long for, that they don't want to be over. Let the children go home dreaming of the story, reliving it, wondering.'

12   www.readit2.org/program/
13   primarytimery.com/2018/02/25/reading-for-pleasure-a-different-king-of-rigour

Writing

'You should write because you love the shape of stories and sentences and the creation of different words on a page. Writing comes from reading, and reading is the finest teacher of how to write.'

Annie Proulx

Writing is difficult. And the reason it is difficult is because when we write, we are transposing thoughts and ideas into something more formal. Our thoughts and ideas might be random or they might be in the process of coalescing and the act of writing forces us to impose some order on them. Writing is formal in the way that speaking and thinking are informal. There are rules to be followed, both structurally and grammatically. There is an element of exposure. When we speak, we are given more license to correct and clarify what we mean. While we can redraft and correct what we have written, there is an element of the public nature of writing which means there is pressure to get it right. 'The act of writing is essentially a meaning-making activity in which writers are creating coherent ideas in the private realm of thought and mapping those ideas into the public world of linguistic symbols' (Kellogg 1994).[1]

As Kellogg notes, 'The task facing the writer is to map in an effective fashion the personal symbols of private thought onto the inscriptions of public communication. This is virtually always a highly demanding cognitive feat. Writers must be able to represent their inner experience, feelings, beliefs and attitudes so that they can be understood in a public forum. This is the crux of the challenge facing each writer.'

When children are first learning to write, they have to learn the rules of spelling, punctuation, handwriting and other mechanics... 'translating ideas into text is a qualitatively different operation when struggling with these low-level production concerns than when they come automatically.'[2] So the physical process of committing ideas into text needs to be practised, so that when the mechanics are in place, the ideas can flow. This is important- the physical and basic processes need to be mastered.

Young children need to cope with the transcription of spoken or thought words into graphemic script, as well as the translation of ideas into written form. Bereiter and Scardamalia[3] note how novice writers need to move from a knowledge-telling way of writing, where the writing is a chain of associations on a topic, to a knowledge-transforming capacity, where the writer can shape the material into a written form which takes account of the needs of the audience and the purpose of the writing task. For young writers, managing this transition is key to the development of their writing.

Good writing cannot be achieved without good thinking. 'Thinking well may not be a sufficient condition for writing well, but it certainly appears to be a necessary condition. One can improve one's thinking about a particular subject by writing about it... Writing in essence is a more conscious process than speaking... but generally writing but the most routine and brief pieces is the equivalent of digging ditches.'[4] However, the good news is that a writer's knowledge of a topic is transformed as a result, converting private thoughts into words on a page. 'Such transformation occurs even when others do not read the text... the

1   Kellogg,R. (1994) *The Psychology of Writing*, Oxford University Press.
2   *op. cit.*
3   www.questia.com/library/1957964/the-psychology-of-written-composition
4   Kellogg *op. cit.*

information collected as part of writing together with the text produced act to change the writer's knowledge and points of view.'[5]

A few words on spelling, punctuation and grammar. This sometimes becomes a cheap checklist of full stops, fronted adverbials and spelling checks. Now, all of these are important, but we need to remember that high-quality literacy encompasses a great deal more than this. Its canvas is bigger, broader and wider than spelling, punctuation and grammar. The problem with the focus on spelling, punctuation and grammar is that these should be the servant of great literacy, not its master. Spelling, punctuation and grammar are the tools with which language is given depth and punch. They are not an end in themselves. If the sector spent as much time supporting children to find their authorial voices as they do to the detail of spelling, punctuation and grammar, we would have more confident, articulate writers who also understand the importance of correct spelling and punctuation. In a review of 'Every Child a Writer', all the pupils interviewed in the sample thought that their writing had got better. However, in all but one class, they focused only on secretarial aspects of writing such as neatness, size, spelling and punctuation. In only one school did pupils talk about what they had written sounding better and using good words.[6]

Similarly, 'Moving English Forward[7]' found that lesson plans and teacher feedback frequently focused on particular grammatical constructions such as connectives, verbs, adjectives and sentence starters. This was directly evident in the writing samples where pupils used these features in their texts, but not necessarily effectively. On the other hand, they also found some schools which provided students with tasks that had practical outcomes beyond the classroom, thus reinforcing the importance and relevance of the subject, but this was not common enough across the survey. And yet, research considering the factors affecting the attitudes and motivation of undergraduates found that assigning an audience boosted students' engagement in the task. So, beyond the importance of grammatical accuracy, writing for a wider audience helps to secure this aspect of literacy.

---

5   Kellogg *op. cit.*
6   www.gov.uk/government/publications/evaluation-of-every-child-a-writer-report-1
7   www.gov.uk/government/publications/moving-english-forward

We need to ask ourselves, who are our pupils writing for? What opportunities are there for authentic writing for a purpose? Some examples: pupils composing letters to parents and carers about a school trip or a visitor; stories going onto a class blog for families to read and comment on; and what about publishing hard copies of their work? All these have the capacity to raise the game, to encourage pupils to do their best work, because it is going to be seen by others.

'Moving English forward'[8] found that 'teacher feedback often lacked focus on meaning and communicative effect. Thus, often the communicative purpose of the writing was lost, or subordinated to, the emphasis on grammatical features, making the writing task more of an exercise in demonstrating usage than act of communication.'[9] If pupils are going to write well, they need to be exposed to a lot of ideas, interesting phrases and language through high-quality talk and reading books. Isabel Beck's work 'Bringing Words to Life'[10] shows how to build vocabulary so that pupils make connections to other words and concepts. She makes the case for identifying words in a story and working through these, both so that pupils understand them and also have access to similar words which provide additional nuance and colour to writing. This does not happen by chance, it is the deliberate focus on vocabulary development which allows children to create their own rich work. And as 'Moving English forward' found, the best writing samples came from lessons where teachers focused on meaning and communicative effect.

There comes a point when teachers have to let pupils just go, without the scaffolds, without the writing frames. And that is scary for teachers and possibly so for pupils, as well. Simon Smith wrote about the importance of support and structure, but also of letting pupils off on their own.[11] And what can we learn from professional writers? Well, it appears that virtually every professional writer struggles at some point in the process. As Gene Fowler said, 'Writing is easy. All you do is stare at a blank piece of paper until drops of blood form on your forehead.'[12] Many

---

8   *op. cit.*
9   www.gov.uk/government/publications/evaluation-of-every-child-a-writer-report-1
10   Beck *op. cit.*
11   smithsmm.wordpress.com/2018/03/26/writing-independently-the-devil-is-in-the-detail
12   en.wikipedia.org/wiki/Gene_Fowler

writers report of writer's block and one remedy for this is free writing[13] developed by Peter Elbow. It is similar to brainstorming, except that the words are written in sentences and paragraphs without stopping. As Ray Bradbury said, 'Don't think, just write.' There is mileage in occasionally using this technique and it removes the fear of a blank sheet of paper. It ensures that the hand keeps moving and can release interesting ideas. Those who use it do not worry about spelling and inconsistencies as these can be corrected later. The spelling, punctuation and grammar are the next stage.

The Writing Revolution[14] is full of strategies to support pupils to become confident writers. Developed by Judith Hochman,[15] it is underpinned by six principles: pupils need explicit instruction in writing; sentences are the building blocks of all writing; when embedded in the content of the curriculum, writing instruction is a powerful teaching tool; the content of the curriculum drives the rigour of the writing activities; grammar is best taught in the context of student writing and the two most important phases of the writing process are planning and revising.

There is also the case to be made for regular writing slots. In Chris Curtis' school,[16] every English lesson on a Friday is given over to writing. Just 200 words with a different focus each week: a structure which is both tight and loose. Tight in that there is a word limit, which is both reassuring for pupils and also places additional demands on them to keep their work concise and loose because they are free to respond in any way they like. This regular practice and sharing of work builds strong, confident writers over time.

---

13 writingprocess.mit.edu/process/step-1-generate-ideas/instructions/freewriting
14 www.thewritingrevolution.org
15 www.theatlantic.com/magazine/archive/2012/10/the-writing-revolution/309090
16 learningfrommymistakesenglish.blogspot.co.uk/2016/11/tell-me-why-i-love-fridays.html

Numeracy across the curriculum

'Mathematics has beauty and romance. It's not a boring place to be, the mathematical world. It's an extraordinary place; it's worth spending time there.'
Marcus du Sautoy

Numeracy across the curriculum is not as developed as literacy across the curriculum in most schools. And there's a good reason for this. It doesn't underpin teaching and learning in the same fundamental way as speaking, listening, reading and writing do. However, there are plenty of opportunities to expand numeracy across the curriculum.

One of the most important reasons for raising the profile of numeracy across the curriculum is that many, including some teachers, say that they can't do maths, don't find it interesting and struggle with it. This is extraordinary and unacceptable. No adult would say the same about reading and writing. So, in order to counter this, we need to develop a culture of celebrating numeracy.

So how to go about it? Well, there is order, pattern and symmetry in every aspect of life. To take the example of the Fibonacci sequence discovered by the mathematician Leonardo of Pisa:[1] in the sequence, one is added to one, making two, then the previous number is added to make three, so that it becomes a sequence of five, eight, thirteen and so on. This sequence is important because it also exists in nature. If we look at sunflowers, the whorls on a snail's shell, the patterns which are evident in storm, hurricane and other weather features, all have the Fibonacci sequence underpinning them. Why is this? Well, that's a good question and could be the focus for discussion and research in art and geography, for instance. It also links to the golden ratio, which underpins architecture and art. By talking to pupils about this, we are exposing them to the wonder and magic of number and pattern, which are inherent in so many subjects and disciplines. This is light years away from making maths relevant in counting out what a shopping trolley is worth. That sort of application of maths, or rather arithmetic, is fine, but numeracy needs to be more than that. This sort of exploration would work well as part of a wider topic in art, science or history.

These are some areas which are worth exploring with pupils: what is the history of maths? When did people first use numbers? What did the ancients discover about maths that we still use today? Who were some of the great mathematicians? There are some great stories about the lives and work of mathematicians. There is a tale[2] of Leonardo of Pisa, also called Fibonacci, for example, who, as a child growing up in Pisa in the twelfth century, noticed that the tower was being built on swampy ground. He told his father and the builders that it would not stay up straight because of the foundations. They laughed at him. But he was right. The Tower of Pisa does in fact lean, as the young Fibonacci predicted. Fibonacci travelled widely with his father and he discovered that it was possible to do calculations more quickly using the Hindu-Arabic system. His work describing the method transformed mathematics in Europe. Now it is possible that finding out about this will stimulate pupils into thinking and wondering widely about the story of mathematics.

When we open up the landscape of maths, we find an endless treasure trove of stimulating knowledge for pupils to engage in. For example,

---

1   en.wikipedia.org/wiki/Fibonacci
2   nrich.maths.org/2468

who first developed algebra?[3] Who invented zero? How did we get our numbering system? What happens when we do this, is we locate the maths in lessons to the wider story. Pupils are likely to go home and talk about what they have found out; indeed, they should be encouraged to do so.

What would happen if we exposed pupils to some of the maths that sit behind computer games or research engines? How might they think of these fields in which they might have future careers? Who are some of the famous mathematicians, including women? Who were Hypatia, Ada Lovelace, Dorothy Vaughan, Joan Birman? As well as Archimedes, Pythagoras, Einstein, Euclid Turing, Ramanujan? Omar Khayyam?

It is also worth unpicking the difference between arithmetic and mathematics. Arithmetic comes from the Greek and means 'the art of counting'. Arithmetic is the branch of mathematics that deals with addition, subtraction, multiplication and division and the use of numbers in calculations. Mathematics also has its roots in the Greek and means 'fond of learning'. It is the study of the relationships among numbers, shapes and quantities. Mathematics uses signs, symbols and proofs and includes arithmetic, algebra, calculus, geometry and trigonometry. And at its furthest reaches, it has the capacity to explain the universe.

What we want to achieve is a context where pupils take delight in talking about number, where they see its potential in many areas of the curriculum, are intrigued by it, while at the same time coming to appreciate that this is not about getting correct answers, but rather considering and engaging with the notion that mathematics underpins our world. We should not regard mathematics as a closed box. Many schools have recognised that it does not stand in isolation and have created 'Maths Trails'[4] which supply natural links to many other subjects in the curriculum, and some secondary schools take part in the 'Cracking the Code'[5] competition. These have the power to provoke discussions and debate beyond timetabled maths lessons.

To take the example of 'Fermi Questions';[6] these were designed by Fermi, an American physicist, to encourage people to think creatively about maths

3   www.khanacademy.org/math/algebra/introduction-to-algebra/overview-hist-alg/v/origins-of-algebra
4   nrich.maths.org/2579
5   mathsmission.challenges.org
6   mathforum.org/workshops/sum96/interdisc/sheila1.html

without being constrained by finding an absolutely correct answer. They involve using different strategies and are helpful because they pose open-ended problems, have no definite solution and promote questioning and curiosity. Some schools ask their pupils this question: 'If everyone in the school ate an apple every day, how many pips would there be by the end of the week?' This opens up questions about who is everyone – does it include the school cat? What do we mean by a week? What is the average number of pips in an apple and so on.

And so it goes on: the world of maths is worth exploring; the possibilities are endless...

SMSC across the curriculum

'Look at situations from all angles, and you will become more open.'
Dalai Lama

Here's the thing with spiritual, moral, social and cultural education (SMSC)[7]: it has been part of education since the 1944 Education Act. It sums up how good schools prepare pupils to live full active lives as part of their community and into adulthood. Many schools express aspirations to be safe, happy places where pupils can fulfil their potential and appreciate others. But it is a slippery element, until we pay attention to what it might encompass. It is possible to consider SMSC through three lenses – the first, in terms of how we do business here: what are the ways in which we approach our work, how are our values lived and not just laminated? This aspect is highly qualitative, but it is possible to gather evidence, nonetheless. The second is, what does this look like in specific subject areas? And finally, it is worth considering how SMSC has an aspect of pedagogy within it.

The elements of spiritual, moral, social and cultural describe those aspects of the curriculum and school life which should be threaded throughout the

---

7   www.gov.uk/education/spiritual-moral-social-and-cultural-development

124

daily practice. They are not add-ons and should not entail additional work – and it is very important to note that the 'spiritual' aspect, which is often hardest to talk about, has nothing to do with making pupils, or anyone else, religious. The inspection handbook[8] refers to the ability of pupils to be reflective about their own beliefs, religious or otherwise, that inform their perspective on life and their interest in and respect for different people's faiths, feelings and values; whether they have a sense of enjoyment and fascination in learning about themselves, others and the world around them; whether they are able to use imagination and creativity in their learning and a willingness to reflect on their experiences. So it is clear from this that there is no expectation for anyone to be religious, rather it is about the capacity to take an interest in others and the wider world.

Pupils' moral development is characterised by the ability to recognise the difference between right and wrong and to readily apply this understanding in their own lives, to recognise legal boundaries and, in so doing, respect the civil and criminal law of England, the extent to which they understand the consequences of their behaviour and actions and interest in investigating and offering reasoned views about moral and ethical issues and ability to understand and appreciate the viewpoints of others on these issues.

The social development of pupils is shown by their capacity to use a range of social skills in different contexts. For example, working and socialising with other pupils, including those from different religious, ethnic and socio-economic backgrounds; their willingness to participate in a variety of communities and social settings, including by volunteering, cooperating well with others and being able to resolve conflicts effectively; acceptance and engagement with the fundamental British values of democracy, the rule of law, individual liberty and mutual respect and tolerance of those with different faiths and beliefs and developing and demonstrating skills and attitudes that will allow them to participate fully in and contribute positively to life in modern Britain.

The cultural development of pupils is shown by their understanding and appreciation of the wide range of cultural influences that have shaped their own heritage and those of others; their understanding and appreciation of the range of different cultures within school and further

---

8   www.gov.uk/government/publications/school-inspection-handbook-from-september-2015

afield as an essential element of their preparation for life in modern Britain; knowledge of Britain's democratic parliamentary system and its central role in shaping our history and values, and in continuing to develop Britain; willingness to participate in and respond positively to artistic, musical, sporting and cultural opportunities; interest in exploring, improving understanding of and showing respect for different faiths and cultural diversity and the extent to which they understand, accept, respect and celebrate diversity, as shown by their tolerance and attitudes towards different religious, ethnic and socio-economic groups in the local, national and global communities.

To consider the 'how we do business' aspect; the sorts of questions we need to be asking are – does everyone feel part of this community? Does everyone have a voice (this is different from having a vote) and how do we know? Are we thinking carefully about inclusion, about how we set pupils, about ensuring wider curriculum opportunities are available for everyone, for instance? Is there a sense of hospitality; that everyone is welcome? Does our school have rules for behaviour which are clear for everyone to understand? Do our pupils have opportunities to make a contribution to school life and the community? Are our values, rules, sanctions and rewards clear and understood by everyone? Are we providing plenty of opportunities for pupils to work with those who have different backgrounds, prior attainment and interests from themselves, and are we taking advantage of the myriad of cultural opportunities in our local area and nationally?

Then to consider specific subject areas; the one subject area which seems to produce more concern than any other when considering SMSC is maths. How, people ask, can I get SMSC out of maths? So, if we are asking pupils to share their ideas, respond respectfully to one another, do some research on an aspect of the history of maths, or consider the impact of globalisation on wages, then we might reasonably say that SMSC is being included. This type of work is going on in many classrooms anyway, it is just a matter of seeing how current practice has deeper links with the SMSC plank.

And of course, there are some subjects in which SMSC is easier to discern: religious education, history and geography all have content which supports the SMSC agenda. However, it is important that the humanities in general and RE in particular are not expected to carry the whole of the

SMSC agenda. It is a thread which should be running through the whole provision.

When we map provision, this should not involve more work. The mapping should just highlight those areas in which we are doing well, which we might have known about; the areas which we now realise support SMSC, and then, when opportunities occur, build in additional links if needed. The point is to bring it more to consciousness, rather than an additional scheme of work. The Diocese of Norwich has produced an SMSC mapping tool[9] which is useful for all schools.

Often, schools are doing more than they realise in terms of SMSC, but they are unconsciously competent and in fact they are doing more than they thought. When we think and talk about our practice, our understanding shifts from unconscious competence to conscious competence. When we bring things to the fore, we are likely to do more of them and embed them, than if they languish as part of our forgotten practice.

9   marymyatt.com/resources

Planning across the curriculum

'Plans are nothing. Planning is everything.'
Albert Einstein

Cross-curricular planning has had a bad rap in recent years. And probably for good reason: poorly conceived, badly delivered plans have often resulted in a muddle. The problem is that there has sometimes has been a misunderstanding of how a theme or topic should work. Without an underlying concept which might be shared authentically across a number of subject areas, the theme is extended to every subject regardless of whether it fits or not.

The second problem with a number of cross-curricular topics is that they often start with a 'wow' day, which takes considerable time and effort on the part of teachers. This would just about be acceptable if the subsequent learning really benefited. However, too often the subsequent lessons do not link back properly to the main point of the 'wow', or external input from a history group, for example. And in the worst cases, the follow-on work becomes a series of disconnected worksheets, with no obvious connection, one to the other.

The third problem with cross-curricular work is that pupils are asked to do something, such as create a model of a synagogue, in religious education. There are several difficulties with this – if the underlying significance of the synagogue for the Jewish community is not properly taught, then it becomes a tired exercise in design and technology. The result is that there are no significant learning gains in either subject. A further problem is that by the time pupils have constructed said synagogue, they could have learnt a great deal more through reading, talking and writing about its significance. And in the same time, they could have produced a worthwhile design and technology product without the thin links to another subject. The bottom line is that the integrity of individual subjects must be preserved.

Now this is a shame, because when done well, thinking about how subjects relate to and support one another can be fruitful. It is better to think of inter-disciplinary rather than cross-curricular work. If inter-disciplinary work is to be done well, it needs careful thought and preparation. The schools who do this kind of work well focus their efforts in several areas: first, they are not seduced by the slick and shiny idea, they ask, does this really add value to learning? If not, they don't do it. Second, they make sure that the links between subjects are authentic – that the art by Holbein connects back to the history, for example, or that a study of Thomas Beckett links back to religious education. And third, they never make the mistake of thinking that cross-disciplinary work is a substitute for absolute rigour and discipline in other subjects, especially in English and maths.

It is the authenticity of the work and its final outcome which is critical to making sure that the project does not drift into the vague and woolly development of skills. The schools who do this well make sure that the work demands high-quality prose, written for a purpose, and is underpinned by an application of maths where appropriate. And finally, that it demands the highest levels of aesthetics and craftsmanship to bring it all together. Some examples of thoughtful work have been developed by schools such as XP in Doncaster[10] and School21 in Stratford.[11]

It is possible to enrich the curriculum by drawing on wider literature, art and music, for example in history, geography, religious education. For example, the West London Free School explains it this way: 'We also want to create a much tighter and more fruitful interplay of substantive knowledge

10   www.xpschool.org/our-expeditions
11   www.school21.org.uk/pbl

across each subject. To give one example, the impact of the Renaissance in both music and art, and within the broader historical narrative. Helping pupils to think across different subjects means they are: (a) freer to do more in-depth and wider work on the Renaissance; (b) quicker to assimilate textbook definitions; (c) more enthusiastic; and (d) more curious about the political and social dimensions that underpin the artistic and musical endeavours. This transforms what can happen in history, or the other way round, of course.'[12]

---

12   The Question of Knowledge – Parents and Teachers for Excellence

The hidden curriculum

'Education is not just about information but also formation.'[13]
Mona Siddiqui

There are two aspects to the hidden curriculum: the first is the way a school's formal work is enacted and the second is the way that it is perceived and experienced by all engaged in it. A school is more than the sum of its parts. The organisation of the curriculum, the wider provision, staffing and timetabling are the nuts and bolts of education. But it is the manner in which they are delivered, arranged and experienced by adults and pupils that is the territory of the hidden curriculum. It is summed up in the phrase 'the way we do things here.' So while on the surface the key elements are the same, it is the way they are enacted and experienced that is the preserve of the hidden curriculum.

Healthy organisations pay attention to tone. By 'healthy', I mean those organisations which are productive over time, are profitable if they are businesses and where all involved in the company, whether as a customer, supplier or employee, experience a congruity of messages and intentions.

---

13   www.bbc.co.uk/programmes/p060zpzg

Such organisations add value both to society and their shareholders. By 'tone', I mean the way they express their key messages, whether these are promotional, informational or in response to queries. At the heart of this tone is the idea that people's opinions matter. This is not the same as acting on every opinion, but it is the case that they are taken seriously. In other words, all those in contact with the organisation have a voice, which is not the same as saying that they are entitled to a vote. And something interesting happens when people believe they have a voice – they become more invested, interested and engaged in the organisation. Now, such organisations pay attention to tone because it is the right thing to do; leaders in these places understand the fundamentals of respect – that no one individual has all the answers and that the greater the power, the greater the obligation to listen.

So, if these organisations understand the importance of the values being 'lived, not just laminated',[14] of making sure that their work is congruent with the decent behaviour towards others, what parallels might there be in schools? Well, we could have the most fabulous, well-resourced curriculum on the planet, but if the delivery of that curriculum is harsh, focused solely on results in public tests, then it is not sustainable. We need to pay as much attention to the 'soft' stuff as to the 'hard' metrics. This is not to make the case for being soppy or unfocused, rather that we need to be both robust and kind. A misplaced focus on the soft stuff means that we do not expect all pupils to engage in difficult work because of a concern about their self-esteem. When this happens, there is the temptation to dumb work down, to narrow the curriculum and for adults to scaffold or indeed complete the work. With adults, this might mean a reluctance to have challenging conversations about standards, because of a fear of hurting someone's feelings.

On the other side of the coin, a relentless focus on the bottom line in business, or results in education, is not sustainable. In business, we have the example of Ryanair, where contempt for customers was part of their branding and later turned out to be the case for their employees as well. And what followed from this was a sharp decline in profits and a subsequent restructuring. When there is a relentless focus on results in schools, it can result in burnt out adults, a distorted curriculum focused

---

14   sites.google.com/contendercharlie.com/www

on teaching to the exam criteria and disaffected pupils. This notion of 'the way we do things here' is the difference between settings which thrive and those which do not.

Sensible leaders understand that if we want to receive trust, we have to trust people first. There is no other way; it does not work from the bottom up, it works from the top down. First, let's consider what it is like when trust doesn't exist in an organisation. The biggest thing that happens is that everything takes longer. Why? Because everyone is second-guessing the right thing to do, rather than going ahead with what they instinctively know is right. Very few people set out to do a rubbish job; most are not lazy and all can recognise the deep satisfaction of a job well done. So when trust is absent, those higher qualities get submerged under the fear of potentially dong the wrong thing. So, for very basic starters, if we want our organisations to be slicker, more efficient and potentially happier, more rewarding places to work, we need to grapple with trust. So, why are some reluctant to offer trust before receiving it? Why is this difficult? Well, it is risky; things might go wrong. Well, what if they do? Most of us are not involved in brain surgery, so if things go wrong, it's not normally life-threatening. So leaders who understand the importance of trust take a deep breath and work out what it means to offer trust. For starters, trust needs to be talked about. It is as simple as saying 'I trust you', 'I trust you to get this right', 'It's not the end of the world if this goes wrong, why don't you try it and see?' So if the message goes out loud and strong that people are to be trusted and that mistakes are not only ok but the springboards for new learning, then leaders in return need to be open about their own mistakes. Not every one and not in every gory detail, but enough to let colleagues know that there is no such thing as perfection, that personal and professional growth come from reflection about what has gone right as well as what sometimes goes wrong.

One of our greatest needs in life is to have our voices heard. It touches the deepest part of our being, when we have the right to speak and be heard. This level of hearing is an affirmation of our true worth. Thoughtful leaders recognise this and they make sure that there is the time and space for this to happen. Yes, even in frantic schedules. They know the power that comes from making sure that the ideas, opinions and thoughts of everyone at every level in their organisation are valued and aired.

They make sure this happens in a number of ways. First, they do it informally. Simply by asking, 'what do you think?' This is paying an enormous compliment to the person being asked. One of the most powerful things we can say to someone is to ask them their opinion. It is a way of saying, you matter; your ideas, your take on this, is important. They do this in private, but they do it in public as well. This sends a powerful message to all concerned that everyone counts, that everyone's voice matters.

The hidden curriculum should be underpinned by respect and trust. At its heart, the curriculum should be done with pupils, not to them. This does not mean that they determine what is taught, rather that their voices are heard and taken seriously. 'One of the most sincere forms of respect is actually listening to what another has to say.'

Section 6:
Leadership

Curriculum leadership

'Great leaders are almost always great simplifiers, who can cut through argument, debate, and doubt to offer a solution everybody can understand.'
General Colin Powell

There are a number of things that leaders need to take into account when thinking about the curriculum. The first is that the curriculum is more than subjects on a timetable; the second is that the National Curriculum is not a scheme of work and the third is that colleagues need time to plan, to collaborate and to reflect. The role of leaders is to know what the curriculum is for, how it is constructed and what content is covered. The work of Christine Counsell in unpacking the key questions to be asked is fundamental in supporting leadership of the curriculum. Her blog posts are essential reading for all leaders, as they consider the quality and purpose of the curriculum in their settings.[1]

To take the first, namely that the curriculum is more than the subjects on a timetable; leaders need to know the quality of the content being taught.

---

1   thedignityofthethingblog.wordpress.com

It is not an easy task to do this with subjects which are not the leaders' own specialisms. This is where they need to trust the subject leaders as specialists and to have conversations with them about what is being taught and the rationale for it being included. This should not be *ad hoc*. It is one of the most important aspects of quality assurance, which will ensure that pupils receive their entitlement to a broad, rich offer. Tom Boulter, deputy head for curriculum, has written about the importance of taking a close interest in the detail of the curriculum. 'We run meetings three times each year between myself, faculty leadership and the SLT link for that area. One of these meetings is dedicated entirely to curriculum at KS3 and involves listening to and discussing the rationale for the specific content being delivered, and the resources provided to students and teachers. My view is that, whilst in the past SLT have not often tended to be involved in discussion of the detail, it's actually a core responsibility of any senior team. If you are a senior leader in a school, particularly with any curriculum responsibility, the day-to-day content being taught in all subjects should be high on your list of priorities to give your attention; it's fundamental to your job.'[2]

The second is that the National Curriculum is not a scheme of work. It might be a surprising observation, but too many conversations about overall planning and purpose refer back to the National Curriculum as though it is the actual scheme for what should be taught. It is the minimum content to be covered and it needs to be translated into meaningful, demanding schemes to bring the subject alive.

The third element relating to planning is the most important, here. There is never enough time. So, given that, what should leaders do to create the space for proper curriculum thinking and planning to take place? Well, the first is to recognise that not everything can or should be done. It is better to start with fewer topics and to do these well and build on them over time. To take an example, if the school has recognised that it has not offered sufficient geography at Key Stage 2, they might take one topic such as India, which is often taught in Year 3, and plan a unit. For the first time of teaching, this could be offered to all year groups in Key Stage 2. Then, in the next round, take another topic and do the same. By the time the original Year 3s have arrived in Year 6, there will be new topics, so they will not be repeating what they have already done. The value in

---

2   thinkingonlearning.blogspot.co.uk/2017/10/improving-curriculum.html

doing this is that several classes will be doing work on the same plans at the same time. This means that teachers will be able to plan together and share what has gone well and what needs to be tweaked, and there will be plenty of examples of pupils' work to compare. Working in this way means that teacher expertise grows incrementally and is consolidated through conversations with other professionals. This is light years away from teachers working in isolation.

If we are serious about improving teachers' subject knowledge beyond English and maths, then directed time should be created for this. A number of schools such as Durrington[3] have overhauled their planning time so that it is focused on subject planning and resourcing rather than administration, which is done by email and kept to a minimum. At Durrington they have prioritised planning time so that it is subject-specific, regular, collaborative and within the context of what is being taught at that time.

Beyond this, in order to create time, there needs to be a long hard look at some of the work such as written marking and data collection, which does not add to pupils' learning. If sensible approaches are made to marking, such as in Andrew Percival's[4] and Clare Sealy's[5] schools, where they take a minimal approach, this frees up time for thinking about curriculum planning. Working to minimal marking not only saves time for teachers, it is more effective for pupils, who have a much clearer idea of what they need to do to improve.

A key thread in this is that teachers should not be planning in isolation. Every teacher with responsibility for a curriculum area should be encouraged to work with others within the school, join subject networks where these are available locally, tap into the expertise of subject specialists within an MAT if they are part of one, engage with the subject communities on Twitter and belong to the relevant subject association.

Here are some practical things that leaders might consider:

1. Providing the time for each subject leader to create a curriculum vision for the subject: what is the knowledge, understanding and disposition we expect to be evident as our pupils learn this subject? Can each subject

---

3   classteaching.wordpress.com/2016/09/19/subject-planning-and-development-sessions
4   primarypercival.weebly.com/blog/no-written-marking-job-done
5   thirdspacelearning.com/blog/why-my-school-banned-marking-confessions-of-a-primary-headteacher

leader describe the subject in their own words? Summer Turner[6] argues that we consider each of these factors when designing a curriculum:

- The purpose of the curriculum.
- Key principles and values.
- Expectations.
- Big ideas.
- Defining the content.
- Establishing the sequence.
- Planning how and when to review.

2. Ensuring there is a curriculum overview for each subject across each year group that is underpinned by the precise knowledge to be learnt. It is important, as Mark Lehain says,[7] to view the entire curriculum as a single project – so that an overarching view of a pupil's knowledge is maintained. The very process of defining and organising desired knowledge at a curriculum level enables a school to present learning in a way that is easier for everyone to understand – and this empowers children and their families to take more control of the process, to everyone's benefit.[8] And what follows from this is that leaders need to know the headlines of what has been taught in earlier key stages and what is planned for later key stages. This is particularly important as pupils move between primary and secondary schools, so that planning takes account of what pupils already know.

3. Providing time for subject leaders to engage in the professional subject community, either through local networks or through professional communities online. There are links to these in the subject section of the book. The subject communities on Twitter are an excellent source of information and debate, as are the curriculum quality marks, and many universities have outreach departments to support curriculum development and enrichment.

4. Ensuring staff meetings and departmental meetings focus on what is going to be taught. At the Durrington School, deputy headteacher Shaun Allison ensures that subject teams meet fortnightly and talk about what they are teaching over the next two weeks – and how to teach it well.[9]

---

6   Turner, S. (2016) *Secondary Curriculum and Assessment Design*, Bloomsbury.
7   schoolsweek.co.uk/ofsted-is-right-about-the-knowledge-rich-curriculum
8   The Question of Knowledge – Parents and Teachers for Excellence
9   classteaching.wordpress.com/2016/09/19/subject-planning-and-development-sessions

In small schools, this will mean taking each subject in turn, led by the subject leader on the key ideas and knowledge to be taught. This meets the criteria for effective professional development: that it should be subject specific, regular, collaborative and within the context of what is being taught at that time. And as Stuart Lock says, 'almost all continued professional development and learning (CPDL) time is focused on subject-specific considerations, so that even when this does reference pedagogy, it inevitably comes back to questions of curriculum. We have twelve 'Teacher Learning Community' sessions that eschew generic pedagogy in favour of subject-specific considerations – these can include professional reading, structured discussion on teacher instruction, consideration of subject-specific blogs or suggestions, or whole departments taking time to attend subject-specific conferences such as those organised by LaSalle Education in mathematics.' Christine Counsell also argues that senior leaders should be encouraging, enabling and rewarding the reading and discussing of subject scholarship within departments.[10]

5. Thinking carefully about monitoring progress: covering the curriculum is progress. There is no need to have complex tracking systems. Teachers should teach the subject, check through quizzes and reteach if necessary and pupils should be producing a final product which will show what they know, understand and can do, as a result of being taught. The use of quizzes and low stakes testing will provide teachers with information about what has been learned and what needs to be revisited. The final piece should be evidence of the cumulative understanding of the pupils and it should be possible to make a judgement about whether they are secure in their knowledge and understanding. Christine Counsell argues that conversations between senior leaders and subject leaders must be cognisant of the curriculum sits behind that data, or else the conversation risks being at cross purposes.[11] At worst, it becomes a conversation that imagines it is about outcomes, but is actually just about measure of outcomes. Stuart Lock, principal of Bedford Free School, once tweeted, 'if in some schools every meeting on data was replaced with a meeting on the curriculum, those schools would have much better data.'[12] If the curriculum

---

10   thedignityofthethingblog.wordpress.com/2018/03/27/in-search-of-senior-curriculum-leadership-introduction-a-dangerous-absence
11   thedignityofthethingblog.wordpress.com/author/christinecounsell
12   twitter.com/StuartLock

itself is the progression model, then numbers change their meaning. Yet one subject differs profoundly from another. And these differences are significant. If SLT are to gain a sense of what kind of data might be useful in establishing attainment or progress, if conversations about matters such as 'teaching' and 'learning' are to have any meaning at all, then the substance of what is being taught and learnt needs primacy. In seeking to establish the quality of the work of a department or teacher, instead of going too quickly to the generic, SLT might more usefully go via the substance, nature, structure and form of the subject.[13]

6. There is no need to create everything from scratch. If the principles of the new curriculum are that there should be fewer things in greater depth and the school is developing new plans, what is to stop a topic also being taught in other years, while the rest of the curriculum is being developed over time? It is better to do a few things really well, rather than trying to tackle everything at once.

7. While it is important that schools create programmes of study, they do not need to do this on their own. For example, the Core Knowledge[14] materials provide a useful starting point. Leaders such as Andrew Percival[15] and Jon Brunskill[16] are sharing their work on curriculum planning and these too can be adapted or used to save time. It is also worth checking schools such as Inspiration Trust, St Martin's in Leicestershire, West London Free School, Bedford Free School and Dixons Trinity in Bradford, who have developed a knowledge-based curriculum. The important thing here is that school and subject leaders consider carefully how they will use resources from other schools so that there is a sense of ownership, even if the school has not created them themselves.

As Tom Boulter argues, this means 'being prepared to question, to have opinions, to play devil's advocate and to challenge assumptions, even when outside of your own subject expertise. It's about moving beyond the requirement to specify content, and towards a willingness to question the quality and appropriateness of the content being proposed: is this the very best that we can be sending students out into the world knowing? Why? What's the rationale to support our view? Whilst feeling slightly odd

---

13   *op. cit.*
14   www.coreknowledge.org.uk/sequencetable.php
15   primarypercival.weebly.com/blog/confessions-of-a-curriculum-leader
16   pedfed.wordpress.com/2016/12/30/using-knowledge-organisers-in-primary

at first, these discussions have been brilliant, leading to ongoing dialogue, change where agreement has been reached, and an overall sense of the importance of getting the choices of taught content as clear, reasoned and convincing as possible.'[17]

In order for curriculum planning to be effective, leaders need to make sure that planning takes account of the research on effective learning; for example, Bjork's work on 'desirable difficulties'[18], which found that if learning is too easy and straightforward, it is less likely to be secure in the long-term memory. The research is now clear that some activities in classrooms result in better learning and it is important that teachers are aware of the headlines of these and consider how to adjust their practice where appropriate. It is not easy trawling the research and this is why it is important that schools support their colleagues to become members of the Chartered College of Teaching,[19] because one of the strands of their work is to make the research available through their website and their termly publication 'Impact'.

Subject-specific continuing professional development has been the poor relation compared with generic pedagogic CPD. However, work by Philippa Cordingley at CUREE[20] has found that programmes that unhand teachers' subject knowledge and/or their ability to teach in specific subjects have a greater impact on pupil outcomes than generic CPD. Again, from the research: 'while teachers in England rate subject specific or contextualised CPD more highly than generic pedagogic CPD, their leaders are less convinced – and both groups see it as much less common and desirable than do their peers in high performing countries.'[21] If we know this and we are serious about raising outcomes for all pupils, we need to make sure that it is given sufficient time in schools.

There are no quick fixes for this. Philippa Cordingley and Toby Greany's work found that many school leaders do work to build strong professional learning environments and systems for developing depth in content knowledge at the heart of school improvement, as the case studies in the report show. But there is a long way to go to make this practice widespread. 'Effective leaders use performance review to identify and balance CPD

---

17   thinkingonlearning.blogspot.co.uk/2017/10/improving-curriculum.html
18   www.youtube.com/watch?v=gtmMMR7SJKw
19   chartered.college
20   www.curee.co.uk/node/5033
21   *op. cit.*

needs for the school as a whole and for individuals. Primary and secondary schools with a strong CPD offer and a focus on how teachers learn through deepening subject knowledge work hard to sustain support and make it systematic, using different kinds of evidence and making sure there is a clear logical connection between analysis of the needs of individual and groups of teachers, school self-evaluation, improvement and CPD activity.'[22]

This is echoed by David Weston's work at the Teacher Development Trust.[23] Findings from the survey of 150 schools showed that access to professional development for teachers varies: 'There is huge variation in investment from region to region, with spending per teacher three times higher in Newham, east London, and Hampshire than it is in Solihull in the West Midlands.'[24] However, the issue isn't funding, because 'Although budgets are tight, there appears to be no correlation between background funding levels and spending on development. Cambridgeshire is the lowest funded authority yet its schools are in the top third for investing in teacher development, while generously funded Westminster schools are in the bottom 10% of areas. There is no simple north-south divide, either. Two-thirds of Hampshire's high-spending neighbouring areas are in the bottom 40% of local authority areas.'[25]

The Teacher Development Trust's research has also found that the most effective schools are planning their development programmes for the whole year. They give staff ample time to prepare and share ideas, try them out, evaluate impact, reflect, and go back for more expert input. By moving from one-off activities to programmes, they gain more buy-in from staff, who feel they have more space to actually embed ideas and make them work. Furthermore, they identified a shift from whole-school professional development to a greater emphasis on teams. Phase, year and subject teams are given more time to meet together. Instead of focusing on administrative tasks, staff look at what to cover next and the best way to teach a topic or idea. Analysis from Brown University found that teachers working in more supportive professional environments improve their effectiveness more over time than teachers working in less

---

22 *op. cit.*
23 tdtrust.org/benchmarking
24 www.theguardian.com/teacher-network/2018/apr/24/if-we-want-to-stop-teachers-leaving-we-must-invest-in-development
25 *op. cit.*

supportive contexts.[26] And it is this way of thinking and planning for professional development that needs to be embedded if the curriculum is to be strengthened.

---

26 scholar.harvard.edu/mkraft/publications/can-professional-environments-schools-promote-teacher-development-explaining

Accountability

'Accountability is the glue that bonds commitment to results.'
Will Craig

There are two aspects to accountability in relation to the curriculum: the first is to be clear about what is to be taught and the second is to have some purchase on how well pupils have learnt what they have been taught. There are a number of audiences when we consider accountability and the school curriculum: parents and carers, governors, local authorities, multi academy trusts, regional school commissioners and Ofsted. There is also an expectation from the Department for Education that the curriculum for each year group be published on school websites.

The headlines on a school's website are the primary source of information for parents and carers. This might be supplemented by the work which their children bring home. Governors need to ensure that all children, including those with special educational needs, have access to a broad and balanced curriculum; they hold senior leaders to account by monitoring the school's performance. This includes agreeing the headlines from the school's self-evaluation and ensuring these are used to inform the school's development priorities. Their role is to work in partnership with the headteacher and senior leadership team to raise standards and improve outcomes for all children.

For maintained schools, there is an obligation to teach the National Curriculum until the age of 16; teach religious education at every key stage; secure access to independent careers guidance for pupils in Years 8-13 and provide sex and relationships education in secondary settings. Academies, on the other hand, do not have to follow the National Curriculum but are bound by their funding agreement to teach a broad and balanced curriculum to pupils up to the age of 16. The Key asked the DfE what a broad and balanced curriculum might look like. A representative said that a broad and balanced curriculum would: comply with legislation; provide a wide range of subjects; prepare pupils for the opportunities, responsibilities and experiences of life in modern Britain; promote tolerance of and respect for people of all faiths or no faith, cultures and lifestyles.[1]

So, having established the headlines of the 'what' of the curriculum, the next question in the accountability arena is how well are the pupils doing? This is the essence: schools need to know how well pupils are doing in relation to the part of the curriculum that has been taught. How they do this is up to them. A spreadsheet with a few key performance indicators and a simple way of capturing whether pupils are where they should be or not, is all that is needed. Complex data tracking systems to show progress are not. Progress on a spreadsheet has no purchase in a curriculum without levels. Progress is measured between key stages through the end of key stage tests. But what we are talking about here is how schools know how pupils are doing in curriculum subjects and across year groups. With levels having gone, it needs different conversations: things like samples of pupils' work; the headlines of those pupils who are secure, those who are not and what is being done about it. This is data being used formatively and it is the only thing that should be done with any data which is captured.

There can be no such thing as 'predicted progress' or 'expected progress', because the current curriculum doesn't work like that. As Jamie Pembroke says, 'Progress is no longer prescribed in advance; instead, each pupil's attainment is compared against the average score of pupils in the same prior-attainment group nationally.'[2] This requires

---

1   schoolgovernors.thekeysupport.com/curriculum-and-pupils/curriculum/
    school-curriculum/curriculum-statutory-requirements/?marker=full-search-q-
    curriculum-result-7
2   www.tes.com/news/there-truly-no-such-thing-expected-progress

more of a sophisticated and nuanced conversation than an analysis of spreadsheets. Clare Sealy, headteacher in London, has described how her school stripped back the collection of data, largely because it wasn't telling them anything they didn't already know.[3] Sean Harford, national director of schools at Ofsted, has also been clear about tracking: 'track' doesn't necessarily mean 'use data'.[4]

Ofsted have signalled that they will be taking a closer look at the curriculum beyond the core and have framed their questions around the following: intent, in other words the knowledge and understanding to be gained at each key stage; implementation, which involves translating that framework over time into a structure and narrative within an institutional context; and impact, through evaluating what knowledge and understanding pupils have gained against expectations.

So the priority for leaders is to be able to articulate the purpose of the curriculum provided in their school, what they expect it to do and how they know whether pupils are successful or not.

---

3   primarytimery.com/2018/03/25/going-data-naked
4   twitter.com/HarfordSean/status/979261121189285889

Section 7: Subject commentaries

Introduction

'In a democratic society which prizes equality of opportunity, the curriculum should be based first and foremost on the knowledge we consider all young people should have the access to and begin to acquire during their school years.'
Michael Young

The section on subjects has been written as a commentary and a reflection on some of the opportunities for curriculum leaders and teachers as they plan individual subjects in the curriculum. A shift in thinking rather than more work. Each section is a panegyric on the individual subjects: beautiful and worthwhile for their own sakes as well as fundamental to developing fully-rounded human beings.

There is a missing aspect to much curriculum planning and it is this: that too little attention is paid to the wider context and the bigger picture. For example, in science for Key Stage 1, pupils have to learn about herbivores, carnivores and omnivores. When you look at what is available for pupils to learn about these important categories, they mostly consist of sorting animals into Venn diagrams based on their feeding habits. There is nothing wrong with this, but it only takes their learning so far. They complete a worksheet, stick it in their book and that element of the curriculum is ticked and signed off as being 'done'. However, in this example, as in many others which take a lesson-led objective approach to curriculum coverage, there is a great deal which is left out. Learning about herbivorous and other animals is more than a worksheet. What would happen if pupils were shown clips or photographs from wildlife programmes and asked to make the same categorisation? What would happen if they learnt more than just the definitions? What would happen to their appreciation of language if they found out about the root of the word 'omnivore'? What if they produced their own taxonomy?

Sitting behind this argument is that they should have access to beautiful materials from which to work; to have the opportunity to reframe their knowledge and understanding; that pupils should be expected to do more than fill in the gaps on a substandard worksheet; that they should be tested on their knowledge after the original lesson, so that it becomes located in the long-term memory.

This section on subjects is arguing both for the integrity of the individual subject and the particular gifts which are available for learning, rather than a narrow focus on completing a worksheet. The questions that leaders and teachers need to answer are those posed by Michael Young: why is this subject worth teaching? What are pupils learning and is it valuable?[5] This section also makes the case for 'powerful knowledge'[6] which, as Young argues, 'has little to do with the piling up and regurgitating of facts. This does not mean there is knowledge without facts, just that facts on their own are not knowledge. Powerful knowledge is distinct from "common sense" knowledge acquired through everyday experience; it is systematic – its concepts are systematically related to one another in groups we refer to as subjects or disciplines; it is specialised and counts on contributions from experts'.

Summer Turner also places the content taught within schools in a wider context: 'the choice and sequencing of facts must be centred in an

5   ioelondonblog.wordpress.com/2017/09/18/what-knowledge-should-we-teach-the-next-generation-the-most-important-question-in-education/
6   Young,M. *et al* (2014) *Knowledge and the Future School: Curriculum and Social Justice*, Bloomsbury.

understanding of the subject tradition. When making a choice about what to study, we are not working as individuals making individual selections, we are responding to the tradition of our subject and inducting our pupils into this tradition. Therefore a subject curriculum must be a response to the academic discipline and our choices of what to teach and how to teach should be guided by this rather than personal preferences. An aim of a knowledge-rich curriculum, in my view, is to induct our pupils into the tradition of our subjects and therefore the great educated conversations.'[7]

Finally, it is worth taking into account Ofsted's review of the curriculum, which is considering the following questions: intent – what are the aims of the subjects within the curriculum including knowledge and understanding to be gained at each stage; implementation – how are leaders translating the framework into a structure and narrative; and impact – how are leaders evaluating the knowledge and understanding pupils have gained against expectations?

7   ragazzainglese.wordpress.com/2018/02/14/pub-quiz-or-published-what-are-the-aims-of-a-knowledge-rich-curriculum

Art and Design

'Every human is an artist.'
Don Miguel Ruiz

To continue the argument that subjects are deeper and more robust if they draw on a wider context, the same applies to art and design. There are three elements to the design of art and design: the first is skills, the second is knowledge and the third is the exposure to art, either through visits to galleries or high-quality images from museums and galleries.

While there is much creative work of great quality produced by pupils in school, there appears to be less focus on the explicit teaching of artists and their traditions. In other words, skills are planned and developed, but there is often less focus on knowledge. There are some schools such as the Medlock School[1] which take a big picture approach to skills development: pupils have regular opportunities to express themselves, linked to a variety of themes using different media and materials such as paint, collage, clay and textiles. Each pupil from Years 1 to 6 has their own sketchbook which moves with them through the school. This provides them with concrete evidence of their skills development, which they apply to a final piece of work. This long-term approach means that pupils have a clear view of the progress they have made over time and it is this which builds confidence to tackle more demanding work.

---

1   www.medlock.manchester.sch.uk/index.php/art-in-school

To turn to knowledge: there are two strands to this – the first is the teaching of artists, their work, context and influence. If pupils are working in the style of Monet, for example, there are great opportunities for them to learn about the range of his output, his life and his legacy. The selection of important artists can be developed into extended research projects. The second strand is spotting opportunities in other subject areas to link to art. This does not mean artificial topic work, rather authentic connections from one discipline to another. In religious education, for example, teaching about incarnation and the nativity opens up multiple routes into art;[2] similarly history and geography can do the same. Again, some schools like the Medlock School realise that art can be a starting point for writing.

Emily Gopaul[3] promotes the use of carefully selected paintings and artwork, which help pupils to make sense of the world when the art they are exposed to is placed in a chronological, historical and geographical context. 'This means that schemes should ensure that the artists, movements and genres that children look at are built upon as they move through the primary years and that pupils revisit key topics in more depth as they get older. Importantly, pupils are encouraged to "read" the stories that paintings tell, they learn how to be "painting detectives" and use the "clues" present in the details of many great artworks. In this way a strong art curriculum can also support visual literacy.'[4]

Emily also has a suggestion for making sure art is part of the everyday classroom: 'primary art lessons often happen in the classroom with class teachers, rather than a specialist teacher, which makes it easy for other subjects to overrun and for art to be forgotten. For schools that find it difficult to dedicate an hour a week to art, teachers should still aim to include short bursts of creativity in the school day. Bite-sized classes (anything from 10 to 30 minutes) could include looking at a piece of art and discussing it, practising drawing skills, or free-flow doodling. Such activities are mess free, easy to deliver and better than nothing when the timetable is tight. Of course, this should not completely replace longer art classes – working for a sustained amount of time on

---

2   www.theguardian.com/culture/2014/dec/05/the-10-best-christmas-story-paintings
3   Gopaul,E. (2017) *Bloomsbury Curriculum Basics: Teaching Primary Art and Design*, Bloomsbury.
4   theprimaryartclass.com/curriculum/art-meaning

creative endeavours is always worthwhile.'[5]

While visits to galleries are not always possible, any school within a city or large town which has a gallery should try and visit. Nothing replaces the experience of looking at the art itself. However, where this is not possible, the quality of the images now available from most galleries is a good second best.

At Key Stage 3, there are real opportunities for developing the range and depth of art study. Here is Stuart Lock[6] talking about the emerging art curriculum in Years 7 and 8: 'Following an exposition of the need to move to a knowledge-based curriculum, the head of art asked me as headteacher what this meant for art and my response was that I honestly don't know. I do know, however, that a great many adults lack the cultural literacy to enjoy art galleries, or even to be able to identify the techniques and media used in well-known works of art. A great many more fail to recognise cultural reference points of some of the greatest works of art throughout history. I suggested that our art curriculum should probably ensure that we do everything possible so that our pupils have access to that which has been handed down through the ages.'

Over several conversations, where the head of art, despite her values, came back to 'what pupils have to do for the GCSE', partly due to the overhanging pressures of accountability, we agreed that the art department should come up with its own version of 'what are the things that excite you, as artists and critics of art, that our pupils should experience by the end of Key Stage 3?'

Following this, our entire art department went to visit a school in London, where the curriculum had emerged from a vision of being knowledge-based, and the school believes that there is a place within the curriculum for history of art. Over the two terms that followed, the art curriculum at CVC has been under constant revision. Where techniques have been taught, they are now taught within the historical context of the greatest or most notable artists or works of art. In Year 7, our pupils are expected to experience, grasp and understand the work of Andrea Mantegna, Andres Derain, Judy Watson Napangardi and Kathe Kollwitz, as well as better known artists Leonardo Da Vinci and Pablo Picasso. They

---

5   www.theguardian.com/teacher-network/teacher-blog/2018/feb/14/art-education-primary-school-creative-industries
6   The Question of Knowledge – Parents and Teachers for Excellence

also encounter Erich Heckel and local botanical artist Evelyn Binns. They become familiar with Pointillism and Fauvism. They study the Grotesques of Notre Dame de Paris and more locally, the Gargoyles of Ely Cathedral.

All pupils produce: a Mandala individual segment; a whole Mandala; a pastiche of Picasso's *Weeping Woman*; a graphite drawing influenced by Kathe Kollwitz; a relief print in the style of Erich Heckel; a botanical drawing inspired by Evelyn Binns and Leonardo da Vinci.

In Year 8, pupils go on to be introduced to works by Giuseppe Arcimboldo, Tessa Traeger, Jason Mercier, Audrey Flack, Wayne Thiebaud, Sarah Graham and Henri Fantin-Latour – specifically the piece *White Cup and Saucer* (1864), which is housed in the Fitzwilliam Museum, Cambridge.

They are explicitly introduced and taught these artists, movements and traditions – rather than 'discover' art that is within them. We explicitly teach them these artists and movements so that they are able to develop and be influenced by, and appreciative of, these artists and movements.[7]

Resources

NSEAD: The National Society for Education in Art and Design[8]
BBC Bitesize[9]
NSEAD[10]
Textiles[11]
V&A Resources for Teachers[12]
The British Museum[13]
The National Gallery[14]
The Tate[15]

---

7   The Question of Knowledge – Parents and Teachers for Excellence
8   www.nsead.org/home/index.aspx
9   www.bbc.co.uk/schools/websites/4_11/site/art.shtml
10   The National Society for Education in Art and Design (NSEAD)
11   www.nsead.org/downloads/START_31.pdf
12   www.vam.ac.uk/info/teachers-resources-for-primary-schools
13   www.britishmuseum.org/learning/schools_and_teachers/resources.aspx
14   www.nationalgallery.org.uk/learning/teachers-and-schools
15   www.tate.org.uk/art/teaching-resource

Computing

'Alan Turing gave us a mathematical model of digital computing that has completely withstood the test of time. He gave us a very, very clear description that was truly prophetic.'

George Dyson

At the time of going to press, the Department for Education[1] announced £79m dedicated to supporting the teaching of computing and computer science to make sure more pupils were able to learn cutting edge skills such as coding, computer programming and cyber security.

The National Curriculum for computing[2] aims to ensure that all pupils can: understand and apply the fundamental principles and concepts of computer science, including abstraction, logic, algorithms and data representation; analyse problems in computational terms and have repeated practical experience of writing computer programs in order to solve such problems; evaluate and apply information technology, including

---

1   www.gov.uk/government/news/schools-minister-announces-boost-to-
    computer-science-teaching
2   www.gov.uk/government/publications/national-curriculum-in-england-
    computing-programmes-of-study

new or unfamiliar technologies, analytically to solve problems and are responsible, competent, confident and creative users of information and communication technology.

These are pretty demanding for primary pupils and are likely to be so for teachers who have not been trained in the last five years. If ever there was a case for professional development, then computing must be top of the list. However, beyond the funding from the DfE, there are plenty of resources for teachers to use, which outline step by step the elements in computing. BBC Bitesize Computing[3] from Key Stage 1, for example, offers clear explanations for algebra, coding, programs, bugs and games amongst others.

And as with other subjects within the curriculum, it is important for pupils to have a sense of the history, the bigger story timeline of what they are learning. So, why shouldn't they learn about Alan Turing and the work he did for the Government Code and Cypher School at Bletchley Park, Britain's codebreaking centre that produced Ultra Intelligence during World War II? Or Joan Clarke, who worked alongside Alan Turing? Or Tim Berners Lee, who invented the World Wide Web and whose mantra is 'let the web serve humanity.' Or Margaret Hamilton, who was director of software engineering for the project that wrote the code for the Apollo Guide Computer for Apollo 11? Or Ada Lovelace, the Victorian mathematician and daughter of Lord Byron? She worked with Charles Babbage on his calculating machines; he called her the 'enchantress of numbers.' At the time, few women studied science or maths, and she is widely considered the founder of computing science and the world's first computer programmer.

It might be argued that the domain for computing is moving so fast that it is important to keep up to speed with the headlines of the latest developments. The resource links below will help teachers keep abreast of the work and resources as they emerge.

Resources

Computer Science Teachers Association[4]
Naace: The Education Technology Association[5]

---

3   www.bbc.com/education/subjects/zyhbwmn
4   www.csteachers.org
5   www.naace.co.uk

Ten tips for teaching programming[6]
Computing at school[7]
Network of Excellence[8]
Barefoot Computing[9]
Code Club[10]
CoderDojo[11]
RaspberryPi[12]
Scratch Team[13]
Hello World: Magazine for Computing and Digital Making Educators[14]
Digital Schoolhouse[15]

6   journals.plos.org/ploscompbiol/article?id=10.1371/journal.pcbi.1006023
7   www.computingatschool.org.uk
8   www.computingatschool.org.uk/noe
9   barefootcas.org.uk
10 www.codeclub.org.uk
11 coderdojo.com
12 www.raspberrypi.org/education
13 scratch.mit.edu
14 helloworld.raspberrypi.org/issues/4
15 www.digitalschoolhouse.org.uk/resources

Design and Technology

'Good buildings come from good people, and all problems are solved by good design.'
Stephen Gardiner

The underlying principle for high-quality D&T is that pupils need to be taught how to design and make things for a particular purpose. One of the issues is that there is confusion about what D&T is and is not – making models of Viking ships or Egyptian pyramids are not D&T; making a moving vehicle to carry an egg safely across uneven ground, or a shelter for the playground to protect younger children from the sun or a coat to protect a teddy bear from the rain are D&T. This is because pupils need to think about what the products they are designing are used for and the needs of those who use them. Good D&T activities need to 'have sufficient depth and breadth to enable pupils to learn practical skills and provide them with the knowledge to make products that move, light up, are structurally sound and don't collapse and meet the requirements of health and safety. Pupils need to be able to test, refine and develop the products they design and make, to check that they work and improve them if they don't. Modelling, drawing or using certain types of two or three dimensional material do not make the activity D&T.'[1]

Where the subject has not been planned thoughtfully, pupils are not sure whether their work is art or D&T. On the other hand, when the subject is well constructed, pupils are likely to say 'D&T is challenging because you have to develop original ideas. You cannot copy something but you have to put your own creative stamp on the things you design,' 'We expect our products to work and they do. Testing and making changes is a step-by-step process,' or 'Sometimes when we have D&T in our heads, we still think about it when we are at home – thinking how to solve problems.'[2] There is a powerful example of authentic design for a real purpose, with pupils from the Wroxham School creating a moving display for a local shop. Pupils take the brief from the owner, are supported by a mechanical engineer and make something that adds value in the real world.[3]

There is also likely to be some hard thinking done in relation to D&T at Key Stage 3. The current model is for pupils to study an aspect every eight weeks or so, and this means they are unlikely to retain much, if any, of what they have learnt. Ross Morrison McGill[4] has argued that D&T should offer pupils fewer topics but in greater depth. He suggests: offering pupils the opportunity to stay with a subject all year; solutions to headteachers to make materials, class sizes and costs easier to justify; using every opportunity to involve colleagues and parents in workshops after school hours to help steer attitudes; celebrating the complex knowledge of the subject with cross-curricular displays and exhibitions; developing projects that recycle school materials and create visible displays around the school; seeking to develop projects within the subject with other areas of the school, particularly with business and core subjects and invites external specialists in regularly to support pupils' experience of the curriculum.

As part of their work on cooking and nutrition, pupils should be taught how to cook and apply the principles of nutrition and healthy eating. Instilling a love of cooking in pupils will also open a door to one of the greatest expressions of human creativity. Learning how to cook is a crucial

---

1   www.slideshare.net/Ofstednews/design-and-technology-professional-development-materials-for-primary-schools
2   op. cit.
3   www.youtube.com/watch?v=Ho0p1GMR4iU&list=PLcvEcrsF_9zLgsF66cQqrahf uogtQHcP5
4   www.teachertoolkit.co.uk/2018/01/13/saving-design-technology

life skill that enables pupils to feed themselves and others affordably and well, now and in later life.[5]

Pupils should be taught to: use the basic principles of a healthy and varied diet to prepare dishes; understand where food comes from; understand and apply the principles of a healthy and varied diet; prepare and cook a variety of predominantly savoury dishes using a range of cooking techniques; understand seasonality and know where and how a variety of ingredients are grown, reared, caught and processed.

The Ofsted subject survey for design and technology[6] found that where the primary curriculum was good, it drew effectively and strategically upon a range of external individuals and organisations to provide expertise, resources and relevance to design and technology. Links with partner secondary schools, particularly, though not exclusively, those designated with a specialism in technology, helped primary schools to overcome shortages in resources or facilities, for example for food technology. Businesses and local organisations were actively cultivated by 12 schools to set pupils exciting and challenging design and make activities, and provided the professional expertise of, for example, chefs, engineers, architects and designers, to support and guide the pupils. Participation in science, technology, engineering and mathematics (STEM) activities also helped eight of the primary schools to develop further awareness of engineering and science. The expertise of parents across a variety of design and manufacturing occupations was sought and used well to support the curriculum. The impact of such specialist expertise is illustrated in the reactions of the pupils.

And finally, the stories behind inventions and everyday objects will both provide a wider landscape for pupils to inform their D&T work and support reading, talking and writing. An excellent range has been collated by STEM.[7]

---

5   www.gov.uk/government/publications/national-curriculum-in-england-design-
    and-technology-programmes-of-study
6   www.gov.uk/government/publications/meeting-technological-challenges-
    school-design-and-technology-provision
7   www.stem.org.uk/resources/search?f%5B0%5D=field_
    subject%3A20&resource_query=Stories&items_per_page=10

Resources

The Design and Technology Association[8]
BBC Bitesize Design and Technology[9]
BBC Teach[10]
How Stuff Works[11]
STEM[12]
STEM Engineering[13]
Design Museum[14]
Ofsted subject professional development: Design and technology[15]
Ofsted: The current state of design and technology[16]

8   www.data.org.uk/for-education
9   www.bbc.com/education/clips/z33f82p
10   www.youtube.com/watch?v=V3PbHwS6CCc&index=40&list=PLcvEcrsF_9zIkMOy
     mmiprE6uSCbnVSOaS
11   www.howstuffworks.com
12   www.stem.org.uk/resources
13   www.stem.org.uk/year-of-engineering/primary
14   designmuseum.org/discover-design/useful-stuff-for-teachers#
15   www.slideshare.net/Ofstednews/design-and-technology-professional-
     development-materials-for-primary-schools
16   www.slideshare.net/Ofstednews/design-and-technology-association-data-
     summer-school-keynote-2015?next_slideshow=1

English

'When I read great literature, great drama, speeches, or sermons, I feel that the human mind has not achieved anything greater than the ability to share feelings and thoughts through language.'
James Earl Jones

Tom Boulter, deputy headteacher, made this observation about high-quality provision in English: 'When talking to some of our most successful students to get their views on how they had learnt to write about literature so beautifully, a recurring idea was that they'd been taught higher quality content than is typical; harder, more sophisticated material that their friends hadn't been exposed to. Examples where we see this in English curriculum planning and resourcing include advanced approaches to poetry, Aristotelian rhetoric, and deep engagement with literary context.'[1]

So what does this look like in practice? Andy Tharby has written about the essentials of great English teaching and he uses the following headings: an

---

1   thinkingonlearning.blogspot.co.uk/2017/10/improving-curriculum.html

understanding that the subject is an inter-connected body of knowledge, teaching is always supported by ambitious text choices, it places great literature at the heart of every lesson, it hinges on subtle and sensitive modelling, places a great value on words and gives students lots and lots of writing practice. And he makes the case that student learning is slow, erratic, associative and cumulative.[2]

It is worth drawing on the National Curriculum purpose and aims for English[3] and rereading on a regular basis. The reason for this is that the delivery of the English curriculum in many classrooms focuses primarily on the written work. Written work is important, it is one of the ways in which pupils communicate their ideas and understanding. But it needs a great deal behind it and the other elements of the curriculum, namely speaking, listening and reading, which are the building blocks from which high-quality writing emerges.

English has a pre-eminent place in education and in society. A high-quality education in English will teach pupils to speak and write fluently, so that they can communicate their ideas and emotions to others and through their reading and listening, others can communicate with them. Through reading in particular, pupils have a chance to develop culturally, emotionally, intellectually, socially and spiritually. Literature, especially, plays a key role in such development. Reading also enables pupils both to acquire knowledge and to build on what they already know. All the skills of language are essential to participating fully as a member of society; pupils, therefore, who do not learn to speak, read and write fluently and confidently are effectively disenfranchised.

The overarching aim for English in the National Curriculum is to promote high standards of language and literacy by equipping pupils with a strong command of the spoken and written word and to develop their love of literature through widespread reading for enjoyment. The National Curriculum for English[4] aims to ensure that all pupils: read easily, fluently and with good understanding; develop the habit of reading widely and often, for both pleasure and information; acquire a wide vocabulary, an

---

2   reflectingenglish.wordpress.com/2018/03/11/the-essential-ingredients-of-great-english-teaching
3   www.gov.uk/government/publications/national-curriculum-in-england-english-programmes-of-study
4   www.gov.uk/government/publications/national-curriculum-in-england-english-programmes-of-study

understanding of grammar and knowledge of linguistic conventions for reading, writing and spoken language; appreciate our rich and varied literary heritage; write clearly, accurately and coherently, adapting their language and style in and for a range of contexts, purposes and audiences; use discussion in order to learn; are able to elaborate and explain clearly their understanding and ideas and are competent in the arts of speaking and listening, making formal presentations, demonstrating to others and participating in debate.

I want to make the case here that the speaking, listening and reading elements should have a higher priority. The reason I believe they don't have a higher profile is because the 'gains' are not immediately visible in the way that the writing is. It is harder to show 'progress' in a misguided view of progress which demands an outcome every ten minutes. What we are talking about here are the building blocks which are both important in their own right and which lead to high-quality writing, over time.

First, to speaking. 'Writing,' as James Britton said, 'floats on a sea of talk.'[5] While much classroom talk focuses on checking comprehension, which is a good thing, it doesn't go far enough to develop pupils' thinking. It is through talk that our ideas become concrete; it is through talk that we can tell whether they make sense or not and we can refine them in the light of others' responses. Without the opportunity to talk about what we are thinking, our written work is likely to be impoverished. Interestingly, it is schools such as School21 who place oracy at the heart of their provision, whose pupils reach standards in the top of all schools nationally, both at primary and secondary. The work of Pie Corbett shows how talking prior to writing raised confidence and the quality of pupils' writing.[6]

The second reason why talk is important is because it promotes the conditions for inference. Too often pupils are asked to infer something from a text, but they do not have enough practice at doing this. The skill of inference is to tease out what has not been said explicitly. We need to pose the question, 'What conclusions might we draw from this?' For example, 'the girl is wearing a fancy dress and carrying a bouquet of flowers.' We might infer from this that she is a flower girl at a wedding. This takes it beyond a statement of the obvious, to a possible scenario. Picture books provide contexts for inference, because it is through the 'reading' of the

5   Britton, J. (1970) *Language and Learning*, Penguin.
6   www.talk4writing.co.uk

image that pupils have the chance to speculate what might be happening, has happened or is going to happen. Simon Smith[7] writes about how picture books help pupils to read between the lines; surely a fundamental aspect of inference. The skill of inference, as Daniel Willingham[8] has argued, cannot be taught separately from a context, because it is always related to the content matter. As a result, in order to ensure that pupils become better at inference, they need plenty of practice talking about what might be going on, even though the writer has not made it explicit. And finally, talk is an entitlement for every pupil. Having one's voice heard is at the heart of confidence; that an individual's ideas matter, that they can be respectfully challenged and affirmed.

Next, to listening. This needs to be emphasised more because at the moment, in many classrooms, the teacher expects, quite rightly, that pupils should pay attention and listen to them. But rarely is this extended to pupils listening to one another. Why is this important? Because it is showing basic respect to another human being and also because it is through listening to others' ideas that pupils expand their own knowledge and understanding. At the moment, in many classrooms, this is implicit rather than being made explicit and I am arguing that we should be talking more about why high-quality listening is important.

Amongst other things, drama supports the development of speaking and listening. Drama is part of the English curriculum; all pupils should be enabled to participate in and gain the knowledge, skills and understanding associated with the artistic practice of drama; pupils should be able to adopt, create and sustain a range of roles, responding appropriately to others in role; they should have opportunities to improvise, devise and script drama for one another and a range of audiences, as well as to rehearse, refine, share and respond thoughtfully to drama and theatre performances.

Role-play and other drama techniques can help pupils to identify with and explore characters. In these ways, they extend their understanding of what they read and have opportunities to try out the language they have listened to.[9] Drama and role-play can contribute to the quality of pupils'

---

7   www.tes.com/news/why-primary-schools-need-embrace-picture-books-boost-literacy
8   www.danielwillingham.com/daniel-willingham-science-and-education-blog/infer-this
9   dramaresource.com/drama-resources

writing by providing opportunities for pupils to develop and order their ideas through playing roles and improvising scenes in various settings. In Years 3 and 4, pupils should become more familiar with and confident in using language in a greater variety of situations, for a variety of audiences and purposes, including through drama, formal presentations and debate. Reading, re-reading and rehearsing poems and plays for presentation and performance gives pupils opportunities to discuss language, including vocabulary; extending their interest in the meaning and origin of words. Pupils should be encouraged to use drama approaches to understand how to perform plays and poems to support their understanding of the meaning. These activities also provide them with an incentive to find out what expression is required, so feeding into comprehension. A powerful way of developing learning through drama is through resources such as the Mantle of the Expert.[10] Tim Taylor has written a beginners guide[11] and Debra Kidd and Hywel Roberts have shown how to work with drama across the curriculum in 'Uncharted Territories'.[12]

The second strand to be developed in relation to listening is that pupils need to hear high-quality texts being read aloud. It is one of the most efficient ways of exposing pupils to language and terminology that are not likely to be encountered in everyday life. If one of the aims of an education is to open up new knowledge for pupils, then reading aloud from texts which are above their 'pay grade' is an important way to achieve this. When talking with colleagues about their views on reading aloud, they agreed that it is a good idea. In primary schools, many have a story slot at the end of the afternoon. When pursued further, it emerges that this slot often gets lost because the time gets taken up with other things. So, as a sector, we are prone to let this slide, even though it has the potential to increase pupil's knowledge and vocabulary. We would never think of letting phonics sessions slip off the timetable. Why? Because we know the difference it makes to pupils' ability to decode text and make the connection between words on the page and the spoken word.

If we are to take reading seriously, we need to expose pupils to texts which make them think, which develop their language and their ideas. They need to be exposed to a wide repertoire of both literature

---

10 www.mantleoftheexpert.com/what-is-moe/introduction-to-moe
11 www.mantleoftheexpert.com/buy-the-book
12 www.crownhouse.co.uk/publications/uncharted-territories

and subject specific material. Sarah Ledger, in an article for the 'Times Educational Supplement'[13] has argued for a new literary canon for Key Stage 3. This serves the purpose of providing pupils with texts which are both enjoyable and will enhance their knowledge and understanding of the world. Similarly, at the Michaela School,[14] their understanding of the importance of reading is exemplified by their placing daily reading as non-negotiable, where they estimate that their pupils read approximately 8000 words a day (2000 of these at home). This schedule is underpinned by silent reading in form time. And the important thing to note here is that this reading is exposing them to work which is more demanding than they would encounter in daily life.

And a few thoughts on reading for pleasure. Clare Sealy[15] has written about how this should be more than the notion that children should love what they are reading, as this doesn't take us far enough. She argues that they should be reading material which places demands on them, either through lexical or structural complexity. Teresa Cremin's research on reading for pleasure has shown that teachers need a wide and uptodate knowledge of children's literature and other texts. This means they need to be given time to keep themselves up to date and should be considered as part of ongoing professional development.[16] And finally, some thoughts on writing: and the first thing to say is that it is hard. Writing does not come naturally. It is tempting to assume that if pupils have mastered mark-making, know how to hold their pencil or pen properly and can write with reasonable speed, then their capacity to write follows. But it doesn't. They need, as argued above, to have heard plenty of conversation, stories and high-quality texts in order to inform their writing. They need to know that SPAG helps their writing make sense. And let's remind ourselves please that it is the servant, not the master of great literacy. There is a link between the amount of reading and the extent to which this supports pupils' writing. The 'Opening Doors' series by Bob Cox uses classic texts as prompts for pupils' writing. It serves two purposes; first to expose pupils to fine writing as stimulus for their own, and second to encourage

---

13   www.tes.com/news/school-news/breaking-views/long-read-why-its-time-form-
     a-new-literary-canon-ks3
14   mcsbrent.co.uk/english-how-should-we-read-texts-in-lessons
15   primarytimery.com
16   researchrichpedagogies.org/research/theme/teachers-knowledge-of-childrens-
     literature-and-other-texts

a love of reading. And The Writing Revolution,[17] underpinned by the Hochmann Method, is a system which enables pupils to master the skills that are essential to become competent writers. The programme enables pupils to become better readers, to communicate more effectively in writing and speaking, and most importantly, to elevate their thinking.

Resources
National Association for the Teaching of English[18]
Team English[19]
National Association for the Teaching of Drama[20]
National Drama[21]

---

17   www.thewritingrevolution.org/method/hochman-method
18   www.nate.org.uk
19   twitter.com/Team_English1
20   www.natd.eu
21   www.nationaldrama.org.uk

Geography

'Geography underpins a lifelong "conversation" about the earth as the home of humankind.'[1]
Geography Association

Michael Palin: 'You can travel the seas, poles and deserts and see nothing. To really understand the world you need to get under the skin of the people and places. In other words, learn about geography. I can't imagine a subject more relevant in schools. We'd all be lost without it.'

If there's a theme running through this book, it is that pupils need to be taught about the big picture and canvas in which they can locate the particular. Let's start with an observation from Margaret Roberts, from Sheffield University, speaking at the Geography Association Annual Conference: 'TV news programmes always locate the places which are being reported, starting with the globe, then moving in closer and then closer still. For example, reports of the 2011 Japanese earthquake and tsunami were first located on the globe, then within Asia and the Pacific Ocean, then within Japan. The location of Japan was significant not only for possible effects of the tsunami around the Pacific Ocean but also for possible effects of radiation leaks. I have never seen geography

---

1   www.geography.org.uk/GA-Manifesto-for-geography

teachers use PowerPoint to zoom in like this to what they are studying, to place it in relation to other places or comment on the significance of a place's location. I rarely see atlases, globes or wall maps used. Locational knowledge of continents, oceans, countries, cities, deserts, *etc*, enables us to place new information into a wider context. I would not argue for the rote learning of this information but students can be expected to know the locations of places they are studying and its significance. If this done for every unit of work, they will gradually build up meaningful contextual knowledge.'[2]

A thought experiment: two classrooms where pupils are studying geography. One, where pupils are colouring in a map of the world: the continents in green, the oceans in blue. That's it. No commentary, nothing learnt apart from colouring in. Next lesson, a map of the United Kingdom with some cities marked up. No commentary, nothing really learned.

A second classroom, by contrast, which is meeting some of the elements in the passages quoted above. In this classroom, pupils are learning about India. Their teacher wants them to develop some map skills and learn about Delhi and the Himalayas. She knows that she can't teach them everything, but she has selected these as a way of both providing a large context and some deeper detail. She wants her pupils to use geographical terms with confidence, so she has prepared a knowledge organiser, which will be referred to and which the pupils are expected to learn and use in their work. She also knows that her pupils need a route in and she wants to include some literacy, so she selects the story of Rama and Sita in 'Seasons of Splendour' by Madhur Jaffrey.[3] The writer and the stories provide the route into the study of India and a flavour of the stories which Indian children are likely to hear. Jaffrey was brought up in Delhi and one of the stories tells the account of Hanuman going to the Himalayas. This teacher is providing an authentic route into this topic on India. Pupils are expected to use maps, information about Delhi, photographs and videos to build up their knowledge. They know that this is important work, because they are going to produce an extended piece of writing which will be shared with other classes. It has an audience, so it had better be good.

---

2 www.geography.org.uk/download/ga_prmghwhatmakesageographylessongood.pdf
3 Jaffrey, M. (1992) *Seasons of Splendour: Tales, Myths and Legends of India*, Puffin.

What we have here is the difference between a fragmented, worksheet-driven sequence of lessons, with no overarching theme or narrative and an extended piece of work which requires research, redrafting and careful thought. As Mark Enser has argued, 'Planning lessons in hour-long blocks encourages a misguided view of how learning takes place. Learning doesn't happen in neat little segments of time; it happens because we are introduced to a new concept, then start to forget it, then are reminded of it again. We struggle to recall, we apply the information, and we make a link between one idea and another. However, by creating individual lesson plans we start thinking of learning as something that has been "done" in that time.'[4]

Does the second example meet the criteria set out above? Will the pupils have learnt some important information about India and be able to produce something as a result?. The overall framework for the minimum that pupils should know is increasingly being set out in knowledge organisers. Andrew Percival's work on the Amazon rainforests[5] is an example of this – once the key concepts and knowledge have been set out, it makes individual lessons more efficient and, above all, more effective.

And some thoughts on fieldwork. It doesn't have to involve far-flung destinations, great though these are. There is geography all around us and our schools. Are we looking closer to home, so that all get the chance to experience the live geography of the locality? Beautifully summed up by Paula Richardson: 'Is it all worthwhile you may ask? ... I can vouch for the hard work, but also the rewards of hearing what the pupils really enjoyed – the night walk in the woods, the high bridge crossing the River Wye, the peregrines on Symond's Yat, the hand operated ferry ... and so on. Peregrines you say, where on earth are they in the National Curriculum? I can tell you, they are in the little pieces of magic those youngsters will carry with them for the rest of their lives. Long live fieldwork!'

Resources

Geography Association[6]

Google Maps[7]

---

4   www.tes.com/sponsored/dfe/what-difference-between-planning-learning-and-lesson-planning-sponsored-article

5   twitter.com/primarypercival/status/972933015839141894

6   www.geography.org.uk/home

7   maps.google.com/help/maps/education

Ordnance Survey Map Skills[8]
Geographical Information Systems GIS[9]
World Mapper[10]
BBC Geography[11]
Time for Geography[12]
National Geographic[13]
BBC Radio 4 'Great Lives', contains many geographers and explorers[14]
'Guardian Eyewitness'[15]

---

8   www.ordnancesurvey.co.uk/mapzone/map-skills
9   www.ordnancesurvey.co.uk/mapzone/gis-zone
10 worldmapper.org
11 www.bbc.com/education/subjects/z2f3cdm
12 timeforgeography.co.uk
13 www.nationalgeographic.com/travel/features/12-books-read-around-world/#cover
14 drive.google.com/drive/folders/1F_ACvc_Rsc1p1lGeegwMpr3eSp4-BT12
15 www.theguardian.com/world/series/eyewitness

History

'A people without the knowledge of their past history, origin and culture is like a tree without roots.'
Marcus Garvey

It's worth revisiting the purpose of study and the aims for history in the National Curriculum:[1] a high-quality history education will help pupils gain a coherent knowledge and understanding of Britain's past and that of the wider world. It should inspire pupils' curiosity to know more about the past. History aims to ensure that all pupils: know and understand the history of these islands as a coherent, chronological narrative, from the earliest times to the present day: how people's lives have shaped this nation and how Britain has influenced and been influenced by the wider world; know and understand significant aspects of the history of the wider world: the nature of ancient civilisations, the expansion and dissolution of empires, characteristic features of past non-European societies, achievements and follies of mankind; gain and deploy a historically-grounded understanding of abstract terms such as 'empire', 'civilisation', 'parliament' and 'peasantry'; understand historical concepts such as continuity and change, cause and consequence, similarity, difference and

---

1   www.gov.uk/government/publications/national-curriculum-in-england-history-programmes-of-study

significance, and use them to make connections, draw contrasts, analyse trends, frame historically-valid questions and create their own structured accounts, including written narratives and analyses; understand the methods of historical enquiry, including how evidence is used rigorously to make historical claims and discern how and why contrasting arguments and interpretations of the past have been constructed; gain historical perspective by placing their growing knowledge into different contexts; understand the connections between local, regional, national and international history, between cultural, economic, military, political, religious and social history and between short and long-term timescales.

There's a lot here and it is demanding. However, there are some underlying themes which should make it easier when it comes to thinking about planning. The first is coherence. Pupils need to know that events in the past are connected to related events at the time and have a legacy, often lasting until today. This means thinking about history curriculum planning as less of a stage set on which certain things happened and more of a chapter in the story which involves us all, up until today. Linked to this is chronology and understanding timescale. Where on the timeline does this period take place and how can pupils gain a sense of what Ian Dawson calls 'frameworks of the past'?[2] Do they have a sense of scale – exactly how long ago was the prehistoric period in relation to the Tudors? Or a sense of period – exactly what is conjured up by the expression 'Restoration England'?

As in every other subject, there is a balance between the macro and the micro, but it is in history that this balance has immense power. It has the capacity to focus in from the telescopic to the microscopic and, in doing so, to build a sense of the continuum between the two. It is the relationship between the grand narrative and the intimate or local story that has the power to draw pupils in. To take two examples of the micro within the macro; Jon Brunskill, in planning a unit on the plague and Great Fire of London, made sure that it included the background to the development of London, the conditions of buildings and streets, a biography of Pepys and the imagined first-hand account of a girl caught up in London during the plague.[3] This unit would convey to pupils the importance of London as a trading and cultural centre of the time, some of the conditions in which people lived, the terror caused by the plague, the contrasting accounts

2   historyattallis.weebly.com/ao1-chronology-and-substantive-knowledge.html
3   Oldfield, P. (2012) *The Great Plague (My Story)*, Scholastic.

of Pepys and Hannah and the impact of the fire. So, an example here of material being taught across the large scale to the personal, from the macro to the micro.

A second example of honing-in on the detail is proposed by Michael Fordham, where he argues for in-depth studies of sources at Key Stages 2 and 3[4] and that these sources should be taught via a 'case study' approach, looking in detail at the sources and how they have been used by historians to construct interpretations of the past. How robust and lively would teaching about Roman Britain be if it included an in-depth study of the Vindolanda Tablets found near Hadrian's Wall? The Vindolanda Tablets are online, with photographs of the original texts, introduction and translations. What would happen if pupils learnt about these in depth? What could they tell about life in Roman Britain and what would be the impact of learning about the birthday invitation from 2000 years ago?[5]

These examples are reflected in Michael Riley's observations: 'I think that the intervening work that had gone on by Dale Banham and others, really thinking about relationship between depth and outline in history has been hugely influential and we were able to build on that by encouraging teachers to think about outline and depth and the way in which they can be brought together across a programme of study as a whole, but also within individual enquiries and the various complex ways in which outline and depth history can work together.' Working this way maintains the integrity of the subject, so that when pupils are asked what they remember about their history lessons, they actually have something to say. That when prompted about a unit on Ancient Greece, they don't respond with 'No, that was topic.' [6]

---

4   clioetcetera.com/2016/12/23/less-generic-analysis-and-more-case-studies-teaching-about-sources-in-schools

5   vindolanda.csad.ox.ac.uk/4DLink2/4DACTION/WebRequestTablet?thisLeafNum=1&searchTerm=Families,%20pleasures%20and%20ceremonies&searchType=browse&searchField=highlights&thisListPosition=3&displayImage=1&displayLatin=1&displayEnglish=1

6   www.history.org.uk/secondary/resource/2594/change-and-continuity

Resources
Historical Association[7]
Gombrich Little History of the World[8]
National archives[9]
BBC archives[10]
BBC Schools Primary History[11]

---

7   www.history.org.uk/primary/categories/curriculum
8   Gombrich, E. (2008) *A Little History of the World*, Yale University Press.
9   www.nationalarchives.gov.uk
10   www.bbc.co.uk/programmes/p059sqrc
11   www.bbc.co.uk/schools/primaryhistory

Languages

'You live a new life for every language you speak. If you only know one language, you only live once.'
Czech proverb

In an overcrowded curriculum, how do we fit everything in? Well, it's tough, but with the right resources it is possible, and no less so in the teaching of languages. This is probably the one area in which most teachers feel they have least experience. In those contexts where there are specialists, there are real advantages for pupils and other teachers. For example, in St James' school,[1] the specialist teacher takes a class with the class teacher at the back. Pupils learn French throughout the school, taught by a specialist co-ordinator. Lessons last an hour and the class teacher sits in to learn the lesson of the week. The class teacher will then allocate an extra 30 minutes to revisit French during the week. So, in effect, pupils receive one and a half hours of French teaching per week. Some secondary schools with specialist provision such as Jack Hunt School work with schools in their local area to develop expertise in language teaching.[2] Their wide-ranging resources online include clips of a teacher speaking French, for example, followed by the translation.

---

1   richmondgovuk.j2bloggy.com/erichmond/a-collaborative-model-st-jamess
2   www.jackhunt.peterborough.sch.uk/page/?pid=162

But language expertise is not the reality for most schools. So how to secure something which is worthwhile, will support teachers and which is not overly burdensome? First, to the expectations for languages in the primary phase. There is no expectation that languages will be taught in Key Stage 1, although some schools do, while in Key Stage 2, the expectation is that the National Curriculum will be taught, by the end of the key stage. How schools do this is up to them.

The purpose of study for languages is as follows: teaching should enable pupils to express their ideas and thoughts in another language and to understand and respond to its speakers, both in speech and in writing. It should also provide opportunities for them to communicate for practical purposes, learn new ways of thinking and read great literature in the original language. Language teaching should provide the foundation for learning further languages, equipping pupils to study and work in other countries.

Pupils should have the opportunity to: listen attentively to spoken language and show understanding by joining in and responding; engage in conversations, ask and answer questions, express opinions and respond to those of others, and seek clarification and help; read carefully and show understanding of words, phrases and simple writing; broaden their vocabulary and develop their ability to understand new words that are introduced into familiar written material, including through use of a dictionary; write phrases from memory and adapt these to create new sentences, expressing their ideas clearly and describe people, places, things and actions in speech and in writing.

So how to go about this? If pupils need to have the opportunity to listen to spoken language and show understanding by joining in and responding, then French nursery rhymes are an accessible way in. The combination of music and repetition make it possible for all pupils to join in. 'Alouette, gentille alouette'[3] which will need some commentary as to why the lark is being plucked[4] and 'Frere Jacques'[5] are good places to start, initially in French and then with the English translation.[6] Once pupils have learnt it, they can be recorded, which means they get the chance to hear just

---

3   www.youtube.com/watch?v=2uWLR-6Zbks
4   www.youtube.com/watch?v=RBZJNJ6_Kvs
5   www.youtube.com/watch?v=LWO-O_cVDcY
6   www.mamalisa.com/blog/frere-jacques-stirs-interest-in-foreign-languages

how good they are. Supposedly simple, but actually containing a range of complex linguistic features such as the subjunctive, these draw pupils in to the pleasure and delight in becoming competent in another language. From confidence comes competence. The explicit teaching of proverbs, idioms and eye-catching expressions mean that pupils have a passion and enthusiasm for learning French, right from the start.[7]

French films with subtitles such as 'Ernest and Celestine'[8] provide a route into the language and a context where differences such as the tooth fairy and the little mouse can be explored. They also help pupils to 'get their ear in' and pick up some of the cadences and patterns of French speech, even if they do not understand it all. These can be watched to get a sense of what is happening and then returned to in order to research some of the phrases and practise speaking and writing them.

The same principles apply to Spanish, Italian and German as well: exposure to the language, hearing and repeating phrases mean that pupils have a sense of achievement early on and it is this which provides the foundations for learning wider vocabulary and grammar. An excellent example of drawing pupils in is 'Telling Tales in Latin',[9] a clever book about Ovid writing stories which introduces pupils to vocabulary and grammar in a structured, careful way. Right from the start, pupils are encouraged to see the links between the Latin vocabulary and words in English. What this means is that, very early on, pupils gain confidence, because they realise that they can begin to make sense of it. And the great thing is that the teacher does not need to know Latin in order to work through the activities with pupils.

There are excellent resources for teaching Latin to young children. Minimus is a Latin course based on a real family who lived at Vindolanda in 100AD: Flavius, the fort commander, his wife Lepidina, their three children, assorted household slaves, their cat Vibrissa – and Minimus the mouse. It is a great way in, not just to the language but to the lives and preoccupations of Romans living in England 2000 years ago.

Schools only need to teach one language in Key Stage 2. However, some schools, such as Medlock Primary,[10] involve younger pupils in foreign

7   mcsbrent.co.uk/languages
8   www.amazon.co.uk/Ernest-Celestine-Lambert-Wilson/dp/B00ESQ7F0K
9   Robinson, L. (2013) *Telling Tales in Latin*, Souvenir Press Ltd.
10 www.medlock.manchester.sch.uk/index.php/languages

language celebrations such as Spanish Week, where they listen to songs and rhymes in Spanish and join in, singing and using actions. Spanish Week is planned as a whole school introduction to the Spanish-speaking world, where links are made in each class to a particular country across the curriculum including PE, music, art, English, maths, food technology and ICT. The school's scheme of work for Spanish initially focuses on speaking and listening in various contexts, such as short conversations or storytelling, leading to whole class performances in Spanish.

Resources

Association for Language Learning[11]
International Language Association[12]
Primary Languages Network[13]
French nursery rhymes: Comptines pour enfants
BBC Primary Languages[14]
Mama Lisa's World: International music and culture[15]
DuoLingo: a free language learning app[16]
Teaching Latin to Primary Children[17]
St Peter's Latin programme for Key Stage 2[18]
Curriculum 2014 Best Practice – Foreign Languages[19]
Goethe Institut: German for children[20]
Spanish Resources[21]
Italian Resources[22]
Latin Resources[23]

---

11   www.all-languages.org.uk
12   www.icc-languages.eu/links/156-the-national-centre-for-languages-cilt
13   primarylanguages.network/home
14   www.bbc.co.uk/schools/primarylanguages
15   www.mamalisa.com/blog/frere-jacques-stirs-interest-in-foreign-languages
16   www.duolingo.com
17   www.youtube.com/watch?v=E1xUtxckbvo
18   www.stpeaton.org.uk/page/?pid=89
19   richmondgovuk.j2bloggy.com/erichmond/best-practice-foreign-languages
20   www.goethe.de/ins/gb/en/spr/unt/kum/dfk.html
21   www.mecd.gob.es/reinounido/en_GB/publicaciones-materiales/material-didactico.html#material-reino-unido1
22   www.lightbulblanguages.co.uk/resources-italian.htm
23   www.irisproject.org.uk

Mathematics

'Pure mathematics is, in its way, the poetry of logical ideas.'
Albert Einstein

Mathematics[1] is a creative and highly inter-connected discipline that has been developed over centuries, providing the solution to some of history's most intriguing problems. It is essential to everyday life, critical to science, technology and engineering, and necessary for financial literacy and most forms of employment. A high-quality mathematics education, therefore, provides a foundation for understanding the world, the ability to reason mathematically, an appreciation of the beauty and power of mathematics and a sense of enjoyment and curiosity about the subject.

The aims of mathematics are for pupils to become fluent in the fundamentals of mathematics, including through varied and frequent practice with increasingly complex problems over time, so that pupils develop conceptual understanding and the ability to recall and apply knowledge rapidly and accurately; reason mathematically by following a line of enquiry, conjecturing relationships and generalisations and developing an argument, justification or proof using mathematical language and be able to solve problems by applying their mathematics to a variety of routine and non-routine problems with increasing

1   www.gov.uk/government/publications/national-curriculum-in-england-mathematics-programmes-of-study

sophistication, including breaking down problems into a series of simpler steps and persevering in seeking solutions.

This might seem highly aspirational and perhaps overblown, which might be the reason why very few of these lofty ambitions are referred to in classrooms. And yet, if we are to see this as an entitlement for every pupil, to have some glimpse of the glory and the majesty of maths, then we need to pay a bit of attention to how we can draw down some of the magic and the mystery of this. It is important that this is regarded as a shift in thinking about planning the curriculum, not about more work. It is not unreasonable to consider how to set the scene so that pupils come to 'an appreciation of the beauty and power of mathematics, and a sense of enjoyment and curiosity about the subject.'[2]

And so, some suggestions for the beauty of maths – literal beauty, as in the Fibonacci sequence, golden ratio, sunflowers or storms and intellectual beauty e.g. the history of algebra, of zero; who were the great mathematicians? This is not to make the argument for these being included in a scheme of work, but point pupils in the direction of the wider landscape, to set them up as homework.

Some commentary on the three elements: first, the principle of fluency. What this means is that children need to have a firm grasp of number bonds, times tables and place value. These are the fundamentals and it is important that pupils know these inside out, back to front and in any combination. Why? Because when these are secure, the working memory is not overloaded, trying to figure out what eight threes are. They should spring immediately to mind. If pupils are not fluent in times tables, it means that tackling problems is much more difficult, because the working memory is taken up trying to figure out these basics and has less capacity for addressing the problem. And it is the same with number bonds; that the possibilities of digits which add up to ten, for example, are secure. This is for similar reasons; namely that the working memory can only handle so much information at a time. And a sense of place value is essential. If a child does not have a sense of place value and is asked, for example, to write down 100 and 1, they are likely to write down '1001'. So, again, this needs plenty of practice. And each individual pupil needs to be proficient

---

2   www.gov.uk/government/publications/national-curriculum-in-england-mathematics-programmes-of-study/national-curriculum-in-england-mathematics-programmes-of-study

in these. Too often, times tables and number bonds are checked as a whole class and that is fine, but it doesn't go far enough. There needs to be individual practice too. One of the most efficient ways for this is through regular, low stakes testing. Dylan Wiliam has commented that the greatest impact for regular tests is when the results are checked and are private to the child. They do not need to be shared with the whole class. But a regular round of the basics, revisited often, will secure these essentials in the long-term memory.

Underpinning this are several ideas: that we need regular practice in order to shift information into the long-term memory; that it is fine to make mistakes, because it is in making mistakes and searching for the correct answer, that the deep learning takes place. Armed with this knowledge, many schools are testing times tables, number bonds and place value through short tests. And once the basic three times tables are secure, these are then mixed up with five or ten times tables within the test. And so on, through the rest of the times tables. And the reason for this is that spaced repetition in an atmosphere of high challenge, low threat, secures long-term retention. Doing this regularly, as a non-negotiable, is what is important. It is simply not enough to say that the whole class can do something; individual pupils need to become fluent.

The second element of the maths mastery curriculum is reasoning. There is plenty of evidence that the teaching of reasoning is the least secure. This is due, in part, to the fact that it is seen as an add-on. But it should not be an option – it is essential. At its heart, it means that pupils can talk about what they are doing, the other possibilities for working out an answer and why some might be more efficient or appropriate in a particular context. It also requires pupils to notice aspects of the maths they are working on, before tackling the particular task. This means that it is important not to go straight into the working out, before thinking about and discussing the key features. This has the effect of slowing down the pace of the lesson, but this is important, as it is through the talk that deeper learning can become secure. So, questions such as: 'What do we notice?', 'What do you expect to come up with, roughly?', 'What makes you think that?', 'How could you begin solving this?' suggested by Karen Wilding[3] begin to open up the space for reasoning. Pupils begin to think mathematically, rather than jumping

---

3   karenwildingeducation.co.uk/math-resources

straight into the question. And it is this process which will help them to transfer their understanding to new contexts, particularly when it comes to problem-solving.

Problem-solving is not an optional extra. It is at the heart of the maths mastery curriculum. This is where the fluency and the reasoning come to life. As a result of knowing the fundamentals and being able to reason about them, pupils are able to apply these to new and unfamiliar contexts.

There are also opportunities for exploring the history of mathematics. In the Winton Gallery at the Science Museum,[4] for example, there are a range of powerful stories about the work of mathematicians in the broadest sense, from salespeople to sailors, aircraft engineers to bankers and gamblers to garden designers. These stories span 400 years of human ingenuity from the Renaissance to the present day, with objects ranging from intriguing hand-held mathematical instruments to a 1929 experimental aircraft.

Resources
Mathematical Association[5]
National Centre for the Teaching of Excellence in Mathematics[6]
La Salle Education[7]

---

4   www.sciencemuseum.org.uk/see-and-do/mathematics-winton-gallery#stories-about-mathematics
5   www.m-a.org.uk
6   www.ncetm.org.uk
7   completemaths.com

Music

'Without music, life would be a mistake.'
Friedrich Nietzsche

'Where provision is good or better, it means that pupils from all backgrounds enjoy sustained opportunities through regular classroom work and music-making for all, complemented by additional tuition, partnerships and extra-curricular activities. Headteachers are key to assuring the quality of teaching in music. They ensured that music has a prominent place in the curriculum and that partnership working provided good value for money.' This from the Ofsted subject report[1] also identifies the following as strong practice; planning for pupils' good musical progression through and across the curriculum by: giving sufficient and regular curriculum time for the thorough and progressive development of pupils' aural awareness and musical understanding; providing robust curriculum plans that identify the landmarks of musical understanding that pupils are expected to achieve, in addition to the range of musical styles and traditions that they are to experience; ensuring that different initiatives, including whole-class instrumental and vocal programmes are planned as part of an overall curriculum vision for music for the school; improving pupils' internalisation of music through high-quality singing

---

1   www.gov.uk/government/publications/music-in-schools

and listening by: taking every opportunity to raise standards of singing work in primary schools, including in class lessons and in whole-school singing sessions, by more effectively challenging the musical quality of pupils' vocal responses; increasing headteachers' and senior leaders' knowledge and understanding about the key characteristics of effective music provision, including the appropriate use of musical assessment and the importance of teachers' musical preparation, so that they can more effectively observe and support music in their schools.

The most effective schools recognised that regular, sustained experiences were essential to secure good musical progress. Schools where curriculum provision was weaker showed limited understanding about musical progression or did not give enough time for music. However, too much music teaching continued to be dominated by the spoken or written word, rather than by musical sounds. Lessons were planned diligently, but not always prepared for musically. Assessment in secondary schools was frequently over-complicated and did not focus enough on the musical quality of students' work. In both primary and secondary schools, insufficient use was made of audio recording and teachers' listening skills to assess and improve pupils' work. Achievement in singing was good or outstanding in only a third of the primary schools visited. Not enough emphasis was placed on improving the quality of vocal work or developing other aspects of musical learning through singing. Singing was a major weakness in nearly half of the secondary schools visited.

Local authority music services made good contributions to the musical and personal progress of particular groups of pupils. However, there were considerable inequalities in funding and provision between local authorities, and between schools within local authorities. Two thirds of the primary schools were participating in 'Wider Opportunities' programmes. However, the length and quality of these projects were variable, and continuation rates were too low.

If there is one resource which is likely to support teachers and leaders in growing confidence regarding quality music provision, it is Ally Daubney's book 'Teaching Primary Music'.[2] Here, there is reassurance and great advice for those who do not have a music specialism; she shows that it is possible

---

2   Daubney, A. (2017) *Teaching Primary Music*, Sage Publishing.

to create great music teaching and learning, even with few resources, as long as it is carefully planned. She makes the point that children already love music; that music in school is multi-faceted and may include music in the curriculum, through the curriculum and beyond the curriculum, for example in assemblies, clubs, performances and playground games, instrumental or vocal lessons and she shows how the subject draws on the richest of sources.

Daubney makes the case for entitlement and inclusion – 'musical learning has many purposes, but one thing is for sure – school is the place where all children must have access to music education, otherwise it becomes an elitist pastime where only children of families that can afford to pay will have access to it.'[3] And, as with other subjects, she has identified the pitfalls of trying to cover too much surface material: 'sometimes, music education seems to block together "cultures and traditions", taking children on what Fautley (2011) describes as a "Cook's Tour", with a cursory glance at different cultures and the music therein through packaging music into short, often tokenistic, units of work. These don't get to the heart of the relationships between music, time, places, cultures and people and do not help children to link up their learning.'[4] However, the range of resources to support the teacher and leader with other specialisms is impressive. What it needs, as ever, is sufficient time for planning, then giving it a go.

Resources

MMA: The National Association of Music Teaching Professionals[5]
New Music Curriculum Guidance[6]
'The Guardian':10 resources for teaching music[7]
ISM: A Framework for Curriculum, Pedagogy and Assessment[8]
BBC Music[9]
BBC Ten Pieces[10]

---

3   *op. cit.*
4   *op. cit.*
5   www.mma-online.org.uk
6   sites.google.com/site/newmusiccurriculumguidance/home
7   www.theguardian.com/teacher-network/teacher-blog/2014/sep/02/10-
     resources-for-teaching-music
8   www.ism.org/images/files/ISM_A_Framework_for_Curriculum,_Pedagogy_and_
     Assessment_KS3_Music_WEB.pdf
9   www.bbc.co.uk/schools/websites/4_11/topic/music.shtml
10   www.bbc.co.uk/programmes/articles/lkxdvCh5p2737xYYFxnShr/about-ten-
     pieces

Jolly Music[11]
Music Mark[12]
Wider Opportunities[13]
Music Teachers[14]
Incorporated Society of Musicians[15]
Arts Council Music Education Hubs[16]
Making More of Music[17]
SingUp[18]
Friday Afternoons[19]
Music Composition Skills[20]
Listen Imagine Compose[21]
The Full English: Folk Music in schools[22]
National Teachers' Choir[23]
Virtual Piano[24]
GarageBand for Schools[25]
UCanPlay[26]

11 jollylearning.co.uk/overview-about-jolly-Music
12 www.musicmark.org.uk
13 www.lovemusictrust.com/about-the-trust
14 www.musicteachers.co.uk
15 www.ism.org/about
16 www.artscouncil.org.uk/music-education/music-education-hubs
17 webarchive.nationalarchives.gov.uk/20141105225609/www.ofsted.gov.uk/node/2364
18 www.singup.org/why-sing
19 www.fridayafternoonsmusic.co.uk
20 sway.com/NT09mj3SybfuBDuH?ref=Link
21 listenimaginecompose.com
22 www.efdss.org/efdss-education/resource-bank/resources-and-teaching-tools/folk-music-in-schools
23 webarchive.nationalarchives.gov.uk/20141105225609/www.ofsted.gov.uk/node/2364
24 virtualpiano.net
25 itunes.apple.com/gb/book/garageband-for-schools/id969094325?mt=13
26 www.ucanplay.org.uk

Physical Education

'Physically educated persons are those who have learned to arrange their lives in such a way that the habitual physical activities they freely engage in make a distinctive contribution to their wider flourishing.'

James MacAllister

'Sana mens in corpore sano: a healthy mind in a health body'[1] What's great about PE? Well, pupils are active and often they are doing their work in the fresh air. Activity matters. It grounds us, makes us happy and helps us to be fully integrated. It reminds us that we are not just intellectual but physical beings, held in balance.

Primary pupils are expected to:[2] use running, jumping, throwing and catching in isolation and in combination; play competitive games, modified where appropriate, for example, badminton, basketball, cricket, football,

---

1   Juvenal, Satura X
2   www.gov.uk/government/publications/national-curriculum-in-england-physical-education-programmes-of-study

hockey, netball, rounders and tennis, and apply basic principles suitable for attacking and defending; develop flexibility, strength, technique, control and balance, for example through athletics and gymnastics; perform dances using a range of movement patterns; take part in outdoor and adventurous activity challenges both individually and within a team; compare their performances with previous ones and demonstrate improvement to achieve their personal best. And all pupils should be able to swim at least 25 metres by the time they leave primary school.

PE Umbrella makes the case that phonics and times tables are practised regularly, and the same should apply to physical education: 'Physical Development needs as much nurturing as anything else that children do in school. We 'rehearse' times tables, spelling and phonics daily, but rarely take the time to work on any fundamental physical skills. Taking into account many children will also be doing little if any of this at home, it's no wonder they are lacking come Year 7. By working in time, five to ten minutes, into the school day and following this program, pupils can begin to construct their own Umbrella of Skills that they can access throughout their school career and the rest of their lives when needed.'[3]

One of the most thoughtful writers on PE and sport is Sporticus, whose careful analysis of research, classroom practice and practical insights are worth reading for all educators, beyond PE. In this example on motor skills and summer sports[4] for instance, he shows how varied practice gets better results. Drawing on a research study with two groups of eight-year-old pupils; one group, the constant, who practised throwing a bean bag at a distance of three feet, and a second group, the variable, who practised throwing the bag either two or four feet away. 'On a subsequent test using the three-foot target – the distance practised by the constant group, but never practised by the variable group – the variable group performed with greater accuracy than the constant group. This result suggests that learning how to modulate the relationships among the target distances was more important for a test at any one target than specific experience, even at the particular target distance used at test. There are many other pieces of research that back this up and it seems to have a particularly strong effect on children.' This subtle but important finding, used by teachers

---

3   peumbrella.com/theumbrellamethod
4   drowningintheshallow.wordpress.com/2015/05/04/motor-skill-learning-research-and-summer-sports

and discussed with pupils, will extend both the physical and intellectual demands on pupils.

Sporticus[5] is also very interesting on the range of content and activities in the PE curriculum; what he describes as 'a mile wide and an inch thick', where pupils are taught a different sport every six weeks. He has identified that more time is needed to develop fundamental movement skills of balance, locomotor and ball skills and has created a curriculum which ensures that time is given to these: 50% split between individual and team sport and movement-based activities. He argues that it is important to do less, but better and for longer, by being flexible with the curriculum, not seeing everything in half term blocks. He makes the case for moving away from PE as sports technique, by promoting play with purpose for numerous benefits. And that it is important to be patient, because motor competency takes time, especially with those pupils who come to school movement-poor. He believes it is important to help pupils find meaning in movement through continued dialogue about its benefits and its place in their lives. Making things fun and helping children to find activities they enjoy are worthy aims, but never instead of learning and the development of actual and perceived motor competence. It is this subtle analysis of a thoughtful curriculum which means that the teaching will develop PE expertise, rather than a Cook's tour of sports.

Primary PE and sport premium provide significant additional funding to primary schools and leaders must use the funding to make additional and sustainable improvements to the quality of PE and sport offered. The funding should develop or add to the PE and sports activities already offered and build capacity and capability within the school to ensure that improvements made will benefit pupils joining the school in future years. The DfE[6] says there are five key indicators where schools should expect to see improvement: the engagement of all pupils in regular physical activity – the Chief Medical Officer guidelines recommend that all children and young people aged 5-18 engage in at least 60 minutes of physical activity a day, of which 30 minutes should be in school; the profile of PE and sport should be raised across the school as a tool for whole-school improvement; there should be increased confidence, knowledge and skills of all staff in teaching PE and sport; a broader experience of a range of sports and activities

5   drowningintheshallow.wordpress.com/blog-index/curriculum-pe-blogs
6   www.gov.uk/guidance/pe-and-sport-premium-for-primary-schools

should be offered to all pupils and there should be increased participation in competitive sport.

Resources

APFE: Association for Physical Education[7]
PE Umbrella[8]
Five reasons why PE is important in primary schools[9]
School Games[10]
Sport England[11]
Youth Sport Trust[12]
The Daily Mile[13]
BBC School Radio Dance[14]
One Dance[15]
Ten Pieces: Time to Move[16]
afPE Quality Mark for Physical Education & Sport[17]

7   www.afpe.org.uk
8   peumbrella.com/theumbrellamethod
9   ukedchat.com/2015/11/29/5-reasons-why-pe-is-so-important-within-primary-schools-by-trainingtoteach
10 www.yourschoolgames.com
11 www.sportengland.org
12 www.youthsporttrust.org
13 thedailymile.co.uk/research
14 www.bbc.co.uk/schoolradio/subjects/dance
15 www.onedanceuk.org/case-studies-examples-delivering-dance-pe-sport-premium-funding
16 www.bbc.co.uk/programmes/p02fr95h
17 www.afpe.org.uk/physical-education/afpe-quality-mark-for-pe-a-sport

Religious Education

'RE is like an iceberg. As you unpack ideas, you come to understand deeper meaning.'
Year 9 pupil

For the avoidance of doubt, religious education is not religious instruction. While there are some who do still equate religious education with religious instruction, this is a legacy of the subject's complex history, since religious education emerged from an instructional, confessional tradition. The resulting confusion in the aims of RE is explained by Dr Richard Kueh in 'We need to talk about religious education.'[1]

The 'material' of religious education stands separately as an object for study, critique and, as such, the personal beliefs of the teacher and pupils are irrelevant. It is every pupil's entitlement to have access to the key concepts underpinning religions and beliefs, whether they are of that tradition or not. All state schools must teach religious education to pupils at every key stage. Local councils are responsible for deciding the RE syllabus, but faith schools and academies can set their own.

---

1   Castelli, M. & Chater,M. (eds) (2017) *We Need to Talk about RE*, Jessica Kingsley Publishers.

Religious education is important because, like every other subject, it provides a particular set of materials through which pupils come to understand important things about the world and themselves. It is the study of religion and beliefs and it stands in the curriculum as a set of ideas and practices which have shaped and continue to shape our world. The business of religious education is an exploration of the influence of religions and beliefs on individuals, culture, behaviour and national life.

As with any other curriculum area, there are concepts and ideas underpinning the subject. The word 'religion' has its roots in the Latin 'to bind', and it is the sacred texts, practices, literature, stories and art that bind communities within a tradition together. The subject includes theology; namely the discussion of the divine, philosophy and the human or social sciences (Georgiou and Wright 2018)[2] and it is through working with these lenses that the subject secures its rigour.

It is important to locate the underpinning concepts, whether covenant, incarnation, ummah or nirvana and to frame the content within these. We know from cognitive science that our brains seek out pattern and meaning, that schemata are fundamental to secure knowledge and that facts are stickier when they are linked to a concept.

One characteristic of good-quality provision is when teachers keep as close as possible to the fundamental 'stuff' of the subject. In religious education, this includes the following: the bible and sacred texts, which should be the beating heart of religious education. Texts have a primacy in that they stand the test of time over centuries, contain the accumulated wisdom of traditions and have a life beyond any individual. They usually point to the ultimate, whether God in Christian tradition, Yahweh in Judaism or Allah in Islam. The texts can provide the lens through which to engage with the theological. Theology is understood here as conversations about foundation beliefs within religions and the idea that a study of religions and beliefs will include some approach to the concept of 'God' or 'ultimate reality' as Georgiou and Wright argue in 'We need to talk about RE'[3]. 'Theology involves investigating key texts and traditions within different religions and belief systems, exploring the ways they have become authoritative for believers and the ways they

---

2   *op. cit.*
3   *op. cit.*

have been challenged, interpreted and disregarded over time[4]

Stories from faith traditions – the hadith in Islam, the lives of the saints in the Christian tradition, the wisdom of the Midrash in Judaism, the Ramayana, are all fertile sources providing insights into religious beliefs. Artefacts should be used as ways of understanding belief and practice. Material based on strong 'socio-historical' grounds, namely that which has emerged from the past, stands up to the critique of time and resonates with society today. It is both static and malleable, in that it can be interpreted through the lens of different individuals and their communities.

Visits and visitors provide the unique insights of lived religions and belief and similarly art and sacred music are powerful sources as ways of understanding and expressing religion.

It is important that teachers appreciate the difference between the external aspects of religions and the lived experiences of individuals. Furthermore, they need to know that traditions differ and scholars often take opposing views. The RE Handbook provides useful summaries of these supplemented by wider scholarship and research.[5]

Resources

NATRE: National Association of Teachers of RE[6]
REonline[7]
Culham St Gabriels[8]
Religious Education Council[9]
RE Handbook[10]

---

4   Castelli, M. & Chater,M. (eds) (2017) *We Need to Talk about RE*, Jessica Kingsley Publishers.
5   re-handbook.org.uk/section/traditions
6   www.natre.org.uk
7   www.reonline.org.uk
8   www.cstg.org.uk
9   www.religiouseducationcouncil.org.uk
10   www.re-handbook.org.uk

Science

'It is important to view knowledge as sort of a semantic tree – make sure you understand the fundamental principles, i.e. the trunk and big branches, before you get into the leaves/details or there is nothing for them to hang on to.'

Elon Musk

One of the main threads in this book is the emphasis on the big picture and the big story sitting behind each subject. Without a big picture, there is a danger that pupils experience individual subjects as a collection of facts, without the underlying structures into which they fit. And no more so than in science. Science is huge. And that's great. But it means that it is very important to provide the headlines so that the detail can be located within a context.

This location of a subject in its historical story is one way of painting the scene, setting out the storyboard. As the story creates pictures in our minds, these support it going into the long-term memory. If we can picture in our mind's eye, the start of the universe, the formation of the earth and the different factors which contributed to this, then as we learn about different aspects of science, we will have that deep sense of cognitive connection. There is real power in 'once upon a time...'

To take two examples; this from 'Sapiens: A brief history of humankind':[1] 'About 13.5 billion years ago, matter, energy, time and space came into being in what is known as the Big Bang. The story of these fundamental features of our universe is called physics. About 300,000 years after their appearance, matter and energy started to coalesce into complex structures, called atoms, which then combined into molecules. The story of atoms, molecules and their interactions is called chemistry. About 3.8 billion years ago, on a planet called Earth, certain molecules combined to form particularly large and intricate structures called organisms. The story of organisms is called biology.' These large timescales are difficult to imagine, so timelines which help to put the origins of life into perspective can be helpful. Tim Urban has produced a series which helps to make sense of just how far back life started.[2] A second example is the Tree of Life Explorer resource.[3] This is interactive and scopes the span of life forms through millennia. This, again, provides a context for pupils to locate their knowledge about what they are learning.

However, timelines only take us so far. While they are helpful in terms of sketching out the trajectory, they can make the subject appear linear. Story provides a more rounded space, which creates the room for the detail within the timeline. The Science Museum Group, for example, has videos and resources to support teachers. They also make available the collection beyond the museum floor so that it is possible to find out the fascinating histories behind even the smallest objects. Teachers can search for over 250,000 objects and archives in Collection Online, take a look at the curator's highlights and discover unique and compelling stories – from objects that have changed our world to the intriguing personal histories that lie behind them. And books such as Bill Bryson's 'A Short History of Nearly Everything'[4] manage to do both, by providing a timeline and the stories within the timeline.

And a reminder of the purpose and aims of science in the National

---

1   Harari, Y. (2015) *A Brief History of Humankind*, Vintage.
2   waitbutwhy.com/2013/08/putting-time-in-perspective.html
3   www.evogeneao.com/explore/tree-of-life-explorer
4   Bryson, B. (2010) *A Really Short History of Nearly Everything*, Corgi Childrens.

Curriculum: a high-quality science education provides the foundations for understanding the world through the specific disciplines of biology, chemistry and physics. Science has changed our lives and is vital to the world's future prosperity, and all pupils should be taught essential aspects of the knowledge, methods, processes and uses of science. Through building up a body of key foundational knowledge and concepts, pupils should be encouraged to recognise the power of rational explanation and develop a sense of excitement and curiosity about natural phenomena. They should be encouraged to understand how science can be used to explain what is occurring, predict how things will behave, and analyse causes.

The National Curriculum for science aims to ensure that all pupils: develop scientific knowledge and conceptual understanding through the specific disciplines of biology, chemistry and physics; develop understanding of the nature, processes and methods of science through different types of science enquiries that help them to answer scientific questions about the world around them and are equipped with the scientific knowledge required to understand the uses and implications of science, today and for the future.

Resources

Association for Science Education[5]
STEM resources[6]
Primary Science Teaching Trust[7] is full of resources and detailed planning to support high-quality science in primary schools.
The Association for Science in Education[8]
Primary Science Quality Mark[9]
BBC Terrific Scientific[10]
NASA[11]
Core Knowledge[12]

---

5   www.ase.org.uk/home
6   www.stem.org.uk/resources/search?f[0]=field_subject:67
7   pstt.org.uk/what-we-do
8   www.ase.org.uk/home
9   pstt.org.uk/who-we-are/partners/psqm
10   www.bbc.co.uk/guides/z22982p
11   www.nasa.gov/image-feature/goddard/2018/hubbles-galaxy-full-of-cosmic-lighthouses
12   www.coreknowledge.org.uk/science.php

St Mary's University Primary Science Padlet[13]
Developing Experts[14]
The Wellcome Trust[15]
Explorify[16]

13 padlet.com/StMarysresources/StMaryScience
14 www.developingexperts.com/
15 wellcome.ac.uk/what-we-do/our-work/transforming-primary-science
16 explorify.wellcome.ac.uk/about